HERBS FOR THE SOUL

Emotional healing with Chinese and Western herbs
and Bach Flower Remedies

TAMARA KIRCHER

photography by Graeme Harris

Thorsons

Thorsons
An Imprint of HarperCollins*Publishers*
77–85 Fulham Palace Road,
Hammersmith, London W6 8JB

The Thorsons website address is:
www.thorsons.com

Published by Thorsons 2001

10 9 8 7 6 5 4 3 2 1

Text copyright © Tamara Kircher 2001
Copyright © HarperCollins*Publishers* Ltd 2001
Photographs © Graeme Harris 2001

Tamara Kircher asserts the moral right to
be identified as the author of this work

Editors: Sally MacEachern and Jillian Stewart
Design: Liz Brown
Production: Melanie Vandevelde

A catalogue record for this book
is available from the British Library

ISBN 0 7225 3926 6

Printed in Hong Kong

Acknowledgments

This book, like most written works, has been a journey. It has challenged me, but most of all it has been a source of great inspiration and joy. The herbs themselves, which grow in my garden and nearby fields, have offered so much healing to clients and those dear to me that it is a blessing to share them with others. Wonder at these plants with their healing attributes must have been the reason for writing the early herbals, such as those of Culpepper and Gerard. Their works have been part of my research, as have those of respected herbalists such as David Hoffman and Anne McIntyre. Great thanks to these practitioners of herbs, and especially to Christina Stapley who has generously given her bright encouragement and wisdom based in rich herbal experience.

To those who made this publication possible, I send thanks for your trust and belief in this book. Belinda, you have been there when I've called for your expertise, and your swift sense of what has been needed has made it a pleasure working with you. Nicky, your encouragement and attention to the details has helped to bring this to a fine completion. And much gratitude to Graeme Harris, for your patience and your unique photographs that bring alive the beauty of these extraordinary herbs.

A special thanks to Aileen for being constantly encouraging and sharing my love of gardens and plants, to Julie for diligently reading each chapter with enthusiasm, to Lis and Sue for your comments on my writing. Dee, Mary, and Carrie, thank you for sharing your tracking on cleansing and clearing, for much of the advice in this chapter is due to your findings and thoughts. Michelle, your belief in my writing and healing abilities, and the weaving of this venture, has opened many windows. Arwyn, bless you for your expansive perceptions and the holding of dreams that are one step closer to being true. There has been much guidance offered with such generosity of spirit from those who touch my soul. Grandmother Caroline, your gentle smile and radiance, your patience, and practical ways, have held me well.

I blame all typographical errors on my cat Sylvester traipsing over the keyboard, but he is forgiven because of his faithful companionship during the writing of this book. You have earned your place on my desk next to the heater. Thanks to MJ for making my time at the computer a constant surprise and keeping me youthful with your excitement for life. And love to Ryan, who is ruthless in making me practice what I preach, and many thanks for making meals when I couldn't take my hands off the keyboard. Clive, thanks for the endless cups of herbal teas, the lunches, and the discussions during those long walks through the fields. May I do the same for you one day soon!

HERBS FOR THE SOUL

All disease is the result of inhibited soul life, and that is true of all forms in all kingdoms. The art of the healer consists in releasing the soul so that its life can flow through the...form.

ALICE BAILEY

HERBS FOR THE SOUL

Herbs have been used for healing for as long as humans have walked the earth. But it is only in the last few centuries that we have limited their use to healing on a physical level. With the coming of the scientific age, we have tended to separate the physical from the emotional and spiritual aspects of ourselves, and so have come to define herbal medicine in terms of physical cures. As a result, we have sought to prove the effectiveness of herbs through scientific measurements. While this has proved valuable and increased the credibility of herbal medicine, it has also diminished the significance of herbs' potential to heal on deeper levels within ourselves.

Disease of the body itself is nothing but the result of the disharmony between soul and mind....True healing involves treating the very base of the cause of the suffering. Therefore no effort directed to the body alone can do more than superficially repair damage. Treat people for their emotional unhappiness, allow them to be happy, and they will become well.

DR. BACH

Now science itself is increasingly revealing the interconnectedness of things, from the vast global weather systems to the intricate balance in even the most microscopic ecological systems. With this growing awareness of our interdependence with the natural world, it is time to rediscover the full range of healing that plants can offer us.

As we seek a more holistic approach – one that brings harmony to the body, mind, and spirit – we can look back to folklore and the traditional ways in which herbs were prescribed to help us understand their true gifts. Old herbal lore makes fascinating reading, giving us different perspectives on the wonders of plants. The herbal knowledge of other times and other societies – often based on extensive practical experience – can provide insights that help us to look beyond definitions limited to the chemical components to rediscover the true essences of herbs.

Many of the conditions that traditional healers sought to alleviate remain with us today, such as melancholy, depression, and apathy toward our lives. And by building on their knowledge we have been able to find new cures for more modern afflictions of the soul, such as stress, anxiety, and boredom.

Each time we consume a herb (in whatever form), not only does it have an effect on our body but its spirit also touches our soul – its healing power is carried through us, infiltrating the cells within our body, the thoughts in our mind, and the sources of our spirit. The life-force within the herb touches us, calming, strengthening, or balancing what the Chinese call *qi* – our essential energy. This enables us to root and grow, and to achieve a more harmonious way of being with the earth.

The British physician Dr. Edward Bach believed that every plant has a certain vibrational pattern, and that many can transform a negative mood into a positive one. His Flower Remedies and other flower essences provide restoring energies for the soul. Like standing under a tree covered in delicate cherry blossoms, or walking through an ancient oak grove, these remedies offer healing power for many conditions, if we can but open ourselves to them.

With the advent of the new millennium, it is appropriate that we reach back to the wealth of herbal wisdom from the past, while at the same time looking forward to what we have yet to discover about plant cures for physical diseases and the remarkable healing gifts of herbs for the soul.

holistic approach

Holistic healing aims to bring a sense of well-being to all aspects of ourself, recognizing the integration of the physical, emotional, and spiritual. It is not a new concept for it is the basis of Chinese herbal medicine, Ayurvedic healing, and Native American plant spirits – all of which have been used as remedies for thousands of years. Even Hippocrates (468–377 B.C.), the founder of the Western tradition of medicine, recognized that different individuals respond differently to treatments, depending on their constitutional make-up.

In holistic healing we look at people as whole beings and consider them in the context of their lives. Diet, physical exercise, and our relationships with others are just some of the factors that influence our health and state of mind. By examining our lifestyle we can become more conscious of our actions, choosing those that are life-affirming and letting go of those that do us harm. Herbal medicine can play a significant role in this process, helping us to achieve a greater capacity to create our life in ways that are satisfying and fulfilling.

The quest to heal the soul means remembering who we are, why we are here, and what truly touches our heart. Through rediscovering this connection to our inner self and to all that is around us, we can rekindle the passion that will light the way for us to bring about the changes needed in our life. Herbs reach out to us, bringing balance and strength to our body, mind, and spirit, and help us on our journey. Once we rediscover our inner resources, we can once again experience the beauty of the world around us.

The relationship between people and healing plants is an example of Gaia, the goddess of the earth, in action, writes David Hoffman, "A unique opportunity is created by the simple act of taking herbal medicines; in making a practical link with Gaia, ecological cycles for healing are activated. The door is open to the possibility of a miracle of healing way beyond the removal of disease. There can be a direct experience of ecological flow and integration, a sense of belonging in the deepest sense, and of knowing that one is home, healed and whole. Such healing goes beyond the treatment of pathologies and the alleviation of bodily suffering that herbal remedies do so well. Rather it is in the realm of the luminous, the transformation that comes about through the divine touch."

herbs and the environment

Herbs are a precious gift to us from the earth for healing. When we look to the shamans, the medicine men and women of indigenous people, we are awed by the sacredness and healing of their herbal traditions. They had a sense of oneness with the world around them. Audrey Shenandoah says, "Being born as humans to this earth is a very sacred trust. We have a sacred responsibility because of the special gift we have, which is beyond the fine gifts of the plant life, the fish, the woodlands, the birds, and all the other living things on earth. We are able to take care of them."

For the shamans, a journey to find herbs is accompanied by prayer and the interpretation of the signs from nature that show the way. As each herb is picked, great care is taken not to destroy the plant, and often a gift such as tobacco or cornmeal is left as a way of giving thanks.

Recently, deforestation, pollution, chemical farming practices, and lack of care and concern for the environment have destroyed many of the places where valuable herbs grow. But now there is a growing awareness that certain areas, such as the rainforest, are rich in healing resource, which is leading to a change of attitude as pharmaceutical companies search for new cures for modern diseases such as AIDS and cancer.

The heart-healing properties of the red hawthorn berries, the strengthening vitamins and minerals of the nettle, and the reviving scent of thyme and rosemary all offer their gifts so freely. As we look to healing ourselves with herbs, we should cultivate a mindfulness that may help to save the planet from an environmental crisis. It is with this vision and prayer

I write this book – that we may look with new awareness to the simple remedies that are so close at hand and cherish them.

western herbs

Herbs are part of the healing tradition of Europe and North America. Despite the move in recent times to the use of sophisticated drugs to cure disease, many people still make use of traditional plant remedies. They are especially important nowadays as we seek gentler ways of healing our ailments.

Plants take up substances from the earth and convert them into vitamins, minerals, carbohydrates, proteins, and fats that our body can use for healing and nourishment. Most herbs have several healing aspects, but one usually dominates and determines its choice as a remedy. The other properties often help the herbs to be assimilated in a balanced way that makes many of them quite safe for us to use. However, it is important to check the Materia Medica (see page 170) for any contraindications.

Combinations of herbs can benefit us by the synergistic way in which they work. For example, a mixture of valerian, passion flower, and hops can be taken for sleeping difficulties. The valerian is a muscle relaxant, passion flower aids sleep, and hops has a sedating effect on the nervous system. Taken together, they make an effective remedy for insomnia.

chinese medicine

Chinese medicine dates back at least three thousand years. In this ancient system, herbs are used together in formulas to strengthen, move, or calm the *qi*, or energy. *Qi* is the essential life-force found in all things. We are born with a certain amount of *qi*, called *jing qi*, which we inherit from our ancestors. As we breathe we also take in *qi* from the air, and as we eat and drink our digestion takes *qi* from the food into our body.

Taoist philosophy maintains that everything in the universe consists of two conflicting yet interdependent energies, *yin* and *yang*. All in the cosmos is born from these energies, which are in constant ebb and flow. *Yang* is hot, bright, upward, and active, embodying the more masculine energy. *Yin* holds the cool, moist, inward, and nourishing qualities that are more feminine. For a sense of well-being, *yin* and *yang* need to be in balance. Chinese herbal remedies address this, so a herb like astragalus (*huang qi*) is used to strengthen and raise the *qi* and tonify the *yang*. Lycium fruit (*gou qi zi*) is nourishing and restoring, supportive to the *yin* energy.

Several specific herbs are recommended by the Chinese as tonics and a number of these are included in this book, such as ginseng and *gan cao* (Chinese licorice). Other herbs, like *chen pi* (tangerine peel), move the *qi*, and are especially helpful for invigorating the digestion. The Chinese formulas, such as Tonify the Spleen Decoction (*gui pi tang*) and Emperor of Heaven's Special Pill to Tonify the Heart (*tian wang bu xin dan*), contain a mixture of herbs that are strengthening and calming.

The formulas contain many herbs that work together to support and balance each other. Traditionally, Chinese herbal formulas are based on the structure of the Chinese court, where a good governing body consisted of several individuals with defined roles who worked well together. A good prescription needs to have several herbs, each performing a role in balancing and enhancing the prescription's healing properties. The formulas consist of the chief (*jun*) herb, which is the main ingredient that addresses the disease or illness; the deputy (*chen*) herb, which aids the chief herb or helps to heal a coexisting symptom; the assistant (*zuo*) herb, which reinforces the effects of the chief and deputy herbs, and moderates the harsh properties of these herbs, or eliminates their toxicity; and the envoy (*shi*) herb, which focuses the actions of the formula on certain parts of the body, and harmonizes the actions of the other ingredients.

bach remedies

About 50 years ago Dr. Edward Bach, an English physician, created a set of remedies that are not really herbs but are based on the essences of flowers, or the spirits of plants. Dr. Bach wrote,

"Disease is solely corrective; it is neither vindictive or cruel, but it is the means adopted by our own souls to point out to us our faults, to prevent our making greater errors, to hinder us from doing more harm, and to bring us back to the path of Truth and Light from which we should never have strayed." His remedies are prescribed for emotional states, as they help to transform negative feelings such as fear, doubt, and impatience to more positive ones like peace, understanding, and forgiveness.

choosing remedies

There are many herbal and flower remedies given in this book. Although most are listed just once in the most relevant chapter, you may choose to combine herbs from different chapters to find the remedy you need. Before taking any herbs please check in the Materia Medica (page 170) to see if there are any contraindications, or precautions, associated with the herbs you choose. This is especially important if you are pregnant, breast-feeding, or on any medication. Please seek professional advice if you take herbs for several weeks without feeling any of their benefits, or if you are suffering from a serious illness.

The Chinese herbal formulas are more distinctive, and require some knowledge of diagnosis. It is sensible to check with a practitioner of Chinese medicine to make sure you take the most appropriate one. The practitioner will probably take your pulse and look at your tongue as part of their diagnosis to make sure the remedy is right for you. Again, check the Materia Medica (page 170) for contraindications and precautions before taking these medicines.

The Bach Flower Remedies (see page 195) are listed at the end of the book, with a short history of their discovery and how to use them. They can be taken alongside any of the herbs and are safe to use under any conditions.

When human beings lose their connection to nature, to heaven and earth, then they do not know how to nurture their environment or how to rule their world – which is saying the same thing. Human beings destroy their ecology at the same time they destroy one another. From that perspective, healing our society goes hand in hand with healing our personal elemental connection with the phenomenal world.

CHÖGYAM TRUNGPA

A journey through the history of herbalism reminds us of the simple and

enduring way in which herbs have sustained and healed us through time.

The different herbal traditions offer a fascinating view of the philosophy

and society from which they have come, as well as providing varied

perspectives on individual herbs. By understanding these different

approaches we can gain a wider perspective on the herbs, and begin to

understand how they heal the soul and support us on all levels – body,

mind, and spirit.

early herbalism

It is impossible to date the exact beginning of herbalism or discover how our ancestors began to use herbs as medicines. Early records, however, indicate that schools of herbal medicine date back as far as 5,000 years to the Sumerians, who described the uses and actions of such plants as laurel, caraway, and thyme.

The first herbalists in many cultures were the shamans or medicine men or women. They developed their intuition and a heightened perception of plants, so that they might understand their healing properties more fully. This deep understanding of the plant world allowed them to communicate directly to the spirit within the herbs. The quest for the right herbs was part of the healing, as the shaman would call for what was needed and then journey to find the plants. Respect was shown toward the plants and prayers were offered in thanks for their gifts. The shamans' wisdom was passed down as part of an oral tradition, so that we can only gain access to it by observing and learning from the native peoples who inherited their ancestors' knowledge.

In ancient Egypt there is evidence that herbal knowledge was closely connected to religion. Osiris was the god of vegetation and his sister Isis held the power of regeneration and brought the gifts of healing. The *Ebers* Papyrus, written in 2000 B.C., describes the use of 85 herbs such as castor oil, dill, mint, gentian, poppy, and senna. Wreaths of herbs were found buried with the dead and paintings of sacred flowers decorated the walls of tombs.

ancient chinese medicine

Manuscripts found in the Ma Wang Dui Tomb Three in the Hunan province date Chinese herbalism back to the third century B.C. References to over 250 medicinal substances were described, as well as their use in prescriptions. Some of these traditional formulas are still widely used today. *The Yellow Emperor's Inner Classic* was also compiled over 2,000 years ago and is a great source of philosophical insights on health, illness, and the relation of the human body to the cosmos. To the ancient Chinese, well-being and disease were related to the seasons and climate, as well as to inner emotions. There was no separation between the energies within ourself and those on a grander scale in nature.

greek and roman herbs

Greek legends add much richness to the herbal tradition. Mount Olympus, where the Greek gods

THE HISTORY OF HERBALISM

played, was covered with a canopy of flowers and herbs that were of service to the gods, as well as to living mortals. The stories about these gods and goddesses clearly show the respect the Ancient Greeks held for the beauty of the plants and their attributes. Many were considered sacred and were used in temples to appeal to a particular deity.

Hippocrates, the Greek physician and "father of medicine" (of the Western tradition), advocated the use of herbs, fresh air, exercise, and good diet. He recorded the use of about 400 herbs to heal illness. Good health was seen to be a balance of the five elements of air, water, earth, fire, and ether. This belief is similar to the five-element theory of China and that of the Ayurvedic tradition of India. Hippocrates stated that illness was not a punishment of the gods, as believed by his ancestors, but an imbalance of the elements within us.

Another influential Greek physician was Galen, who expanded on Hippocrates' philosophy. His work *De Simplicibus* became the standard medical text in Rome, and later of Arab physicians and medieval monks. *De Materia Medica*, written in the first century A.D. by the Greek physician Dioscorides, provided a major source of herbal knowledge for the next 1,500 years. Dioscorides worked as a physician, serving the Roman emperor Nero's armies, collecting information on many herbs such as balm, basil, coriander, fennel, garlic, and rosemary.

It was the Roman armies that were responsible for spreading herbal lore throughout Europe, as they brought many of their medicinal plants with them on their conquests. Pliny the Elder (A.D. 23–79) was a Roman naturalist who collected an encyclopedia of herbal knowledge called *Naturalis Historia*. However, with the advent of Christianity, the Church considered that *it* should be responsible for the health of the mind and the soul, and so it started to repress the use of many "pagan" herbs.

medieval monasteries

The manuscripts of Hippocrates and Dioscorides were preserved in monasteries, where they were translated and copied by diligent monks. Herb and flower gardens were grown in the grounds of abbeys and monasteries, and they became local centers of herbal treatment. Among the common people, the folk tradition of herbs was passed on through midwives or "wise women." However, fear and superstition meant that many women healers were persecuted as witches, and much of the herbal wisdom from this time has been lost.

The Renaissance saw a revival in herbalism and a search for new interpretations of the healing plants. The German alchemist Paracelsus wrote about the doctrine of signatures, in which any herb valued for its medicinal properties was said to be imprinted with a clear sign from God in its structure and in the way that it grew. Lungwort, for example, had spotted leaves that were said to resemble diseased lungs, and was thus indicated for respiratory conditions; walnuts resembled the brain and so were thought to assist mental activity; and the little blue flower of eyebright with its yellow center suggested healing properties for the eyes.

In 1597 John Gerard wrote *The Herbal*, containing herbal information in English. This made it accessible to women who gathered herbs for the household and to apothecaries, whereas herbal knowledge had previously been restricted to educated physicians who understood Latin. Nicholas Culpepper, born in London in 1616, combined his interest in astrology with his knowledge of herbs. Linking plants with the stars and planets was not a new concept, however, as Hippocrates had also studied astronomy.

modern herbalism

The French philosopher René Descartes (1596–1650) believed that mind, body, and nature worked separately. This philosophy was the foundation of a new age of medicine. Scientific discoveries led to a division between the anatomy and physiology of the body and the more spiritual aspects of the soul. Through the centuries a

handful of traditional herbalists tried to maintain a holistic outlook, but by the 19th century the chemical composition of herbs was being analyzed to discover their effects on the physical body. Many herbs subsequently became the basis of modern medicines. The pain-relieving properties of willow, for instance, have been used in aspirin.

Mrs M. Grieves wrote *A Modern Herbal* in 1931, a collection of herbal wisdom, historical anecdotes, and recipes for the kitchen. She also included her monographs of herbs and flowers, most of which grew in her garden. This comprehensive and delightful book was edited by Mrs Leyel, who was the founder and director of the British Society for Herbalists. Its simplicity and practicality rekindles the excitement and wisdom of herbal traditions.

Despite the many advances of modern medicine, there is still a demand for herbal medicine. Many people have experienced how effective plant remedies can be for a range of ailments, and interest in herbalism continues to grow. Perhaps this is because of our curiosity to know more about the medicinal properties of the plants that grow in our gardens, or maybe it is because we seek to rediscover our connection to living forces within the Earth herself through the healing and beauty of her plants.

HERBS
THAT
INVITE
PEACE AND
STILLNESS

Today, there is an urgent quest for peace – for peace within ourselves and our society, as well as among different countries, cultures, and religions. Yet peace is elusive, while chaos and violence seem ever on the increase, not only in reality but also in the fictional events portrayed by the entertainment media.

It is in the silence of the heart that God speaks.
MOTHER TERESA

HERBS THAT INVITE PEACE AND STILLNESS

Our society is fast, stimulating, and demanding. There is continual pressure to succeed at work, both financially and in terms of advancement. Family life is often a precarious balance, especially if both parents are working. Although there is greater freedom to create a role for ourselves that is exciting and challenging, we can become overwhelmed by the many options available to us. We feel we are letting ourselves and others down if we do not achieve it "all."

A good place to begin our global quest for peace is within ourselves. When we are under strain and stress our bodies do not function efficiently. Our minds can get caught in confusion and indecision. The spirit becomes weary and we lose our delight in life. Inner peace takes us back to our soul, so we may recover our strength, and remember who we are.

Just as a knowledge of what is right and wrong informs the quest for world peace, so our own ethics enable us to act in a way that is true to ourselves, not according to someone else's demands. When we know in our heart that we have acted according to our own truths and values, we are closer to finding peace within ourselves. Each time we are challenged we have an opportunity to choose the right action that will bring us closer to truly "being our beliefs." Although this is not always easy, it brings a sense of peace.

The Dalai Lama, a spiritual leader of

the Buddhist faith, speaks of finding peace through compassion for ourselves and others. The Dalai Lama says, "Compassion can be roughly defined in terms of a state of mind that is non-violent, nonharming and nonaggressive. It is a mental attitude based on the wish for others to be free from suffering and is associated with a sense of commitment, responsibility, and respect towards others. In discussing the definition of compassion, the Tibetan word 'Tse-wa', there is a sense to the word of its being a state of mind that can include a wish for good things for oneself. In developing compassion, perhaps one could begin with the wish that oneself be free of suffering and then take it and extend it out to include and embrace others."

Compassion allows us to accept the mistakes and flaws that are part of who we are. In accepting and understanding our own humanity, we can begin to let go of anger, guilt, and blame. We can accept and understand others, and begin to find a way of healing the wounds and rifts that keep us from truly being at peace.

Reaching out to help others can bring what is needed to heal ourselves.

By taking good care of the present moment, we take good care for the future. Working for peace in the future is to work for peace in the present moment.
THICH NHAT HANH

Holding a quiet space within enables us to hear what someone else needs. By putting aside our own wants and problems, we are able to focus on others, and we may find that in the support and advice we give to others is what we were looking for ourselves. We might even begin to laugh at the synchronicity of life.

When we are quiet within ourselves, we can find a still point where we can contact our intuition. Here we gather in all of our knowledge and wisdom to help us decide what is the next step forward. We remember that we have survived many injustices and hurts, and recall the times from our past when we had the courage and strength to cope. In this place we let go of the tensions and negative emotions that distract us from that which gives meaning to our lives. We find an oasis, a place of tranquility, to refresh and renew us.

The herbs described in this chapter help us to find an inner peace through calming the mind and easing tensions in the body and so nourish and replenish the soul.

Before using any of the herbs, check the Materia Medica (*page 170*) for dosages and any contraindications.

3

VALERIAN

WESTERN HERBS

valeriana officinalis

The name of this herb is derived from the Latin *valere*, meaning "to be in health." It reduces tension and anxiety and is a good pain reliever for tension headaches and migraines. As an antispasmodic, it helps to relax painful gut ache and can be used to ease tight, knotted muscles.

During the Second World War valerian was used for treating shell shock and nervous stress in soldiers and was said to be especially effective in calming the nerves of civilians during air raids. Nowadays it is still used for chronic weakness of the nervous system, to help soothe nerves that are on edge. Its releasing action helps to free energy held within the body due to shock and trauma.

For over 2,000 years valerian has been used for promoting clarity of thought and good eyesight. Today it still has a valuable role to play as a remedy for memory loss, long-term mental depression, and poor vision. It can also be used to treat mild cases of insomnia.

There is one problem with valerian – it is very "fragrant" when cooked. The smell is said to be similar to ancient leather or stale perspiration. Fortunately the tincture does not smell as bad, but it still has a very noticeable odor. You can add the root to soups, stews, and stuffings, as well as to a relaxing drink.

Passiflora, or passion flower, is so named because the corona in the flower's center resembles the crown of thorns worn by Jesus Christ. The other parts of the flower are said to be the instruments of the Passion of Christ. It is a most beautiful and unusual flower that delights all who see it with its uniqueness, bringing joy to the soul.

WESTERN HERBS

PASSION FLOWER

passiflora incarnata

This herb is an excellent treatment for insomnia, whether this is due to overwork or exhaustion. It combines well with valerian and hops to help bring on a restful sleep. It eases nerve pain, such as neuralgia and shingles, and helps to ease the symptoms of withdrawal from antidepressants.

Skullcap is a nourishing tonic for the nerves, widely used as a herbal treatment for stress and anxiety. Rich in minerals necessary for a healthy nervous system, it relaxes while at the same time renewing and strengthening. It is a reliable remedy for tension headaches, neuralgia, and breakdowns caused by nervous exhaustion. Agitation, anxiety, hysteria, and depression will all be helped by taking this remedy.

WESTERN HERBS

SKULLCAP

scutellaria laterifolia

Combining skullcap with hormone-balancing herbs such as *Vitex agnus castus* and motherwort, will help with insomnia and depression during menopause and ease symptoms of premenstrual tension.

Skullcap is an essential part of treatment for withdrawal from tranquilizers and anti-depressants. It lifts the spirit, pacifying the everyday tensions and agitations that throw us out of balance.

This twining vine with heart-shaped leaves and yellow-green flowers grows wild around trees and through hedgerows. Its name comes from the Anglo-Saxon 'hoppan', meaning to climb. It curls clock-wise around tree trunks, clinging to them with tiny barbs. The larger female blooms contain the substances used in beer-brewing and herbal medicine.

WESTERN HERBS

HOPS

humulus lupulus

A soothing remedy, hops ease cramps and spasms, and is especially helpful for digestive complaints. The bitters in hops aid this system and encourage the secretion of digestive juices. Traditionally, hops were infused in sherry to make a good digestive cordial and brewed into a herb beer.

Hops have a sedating and pain-relieving action and has been smoked for its narcotic properties. It has a relaxing effect that brings a restful and restoring sense of ease. Combined with valerian and passion flower, hops are especially useful for conditions of high anxiety and sleeplessness and has been used in sleep pillows. It is not a nerve tonic so, unlike skullcap, it would not be appropriate in cases of nervous exhaustion. Avoid using hops if there are signs of depression.

Dill grows wild in the warm Mediterranean, and is becoming more popular here. It is mentioned in St. Matthew, under its Greek name of *anethon* (wrongly transcribed as anise by English translators in 1380). Dill was commonly used in cooking, brewing, and pickling during the Middle Ages. It was also used by magicians in their spells and charms, especially to guard against witchcraft. Culpepper tells us that "Mercury has the dominion of this plant, and therefore to be sure it strengthens the brain...."

WESTERN HERBS

DILL

anethum graveolens

Our name for this herb is derived, according to Prior's *Popular Names of English Plants*, from the old Norse word dilla, which means to lull. It is used, appropriately, to treat colic and ease wind and digestive discomfort in babies, as well as to calm them. Dill is rich in volatile oils that stimulate the movement of the digestive system and relax the stomach.

Digestion is a key factor in maintaining good health and a sense of well-being. When our digestion is working properly, without discomfort, we feel well. However, slight niggling pains in the stomach and guts can cause irritability. At such times, drinking a tea made from crushed seeds of dill and a little honey will comfort and soothe body and mind.

CATMINT

nepeta cataria

Catmint has a gentle effect and is an excellent remedy for babies or children with troubled sleep. It grows wild on wastelands and dry banks, and has become popular as a cottage garden plant. It has a small, fine, pale flower and a gray-green, soft, downy leaf. Catmint is sometimes called catnip because of its scent, which is attractive to cats.

Catmint has a long-standing reputation as a valuable medicinal herb for treating many conditions. It is a traditional cold and flu remedy which cools feverish conditions and trembling. As a carminative (expelling gas from the digestive system) with antispasmodic properties, it can be used like dill for gastric upsets and flatulence. It is also an astringent, so is a good remedy for the treatment of diarrhea, especially in children. It also has a sedative or relaxing effect on the nervous system.

Grieves says, "Catnep Tea is a valuable drink in every case of fever, because of its action of inducing sleep and producing perspiration without increasing the heat within the system. It is good in restlessness, colic, insanity and nervousness, and is used as a mild nervine for children....The infusion of 1 oz. to a pint of boiling water may be taken by adults in doses of 2 tablespoonful, by children 2 to 3 teaspoonfuls frequently, to relieve pain and flatulence.... "

ROSES

The fragrance and the beauty of the rose appeal to lovers. For centuries poetry, stories, and songs have described and praised its virtues. But its herbal properties have been much neglected; the high price of the flowers and the difficulty of obtaining rose tincture are partly to blame.

The rose has a long tradition in the courting and wooing of lovers. It not only plays a part in seduction, however, it also benefits the reproductive system, treating infertility, impotence, and low sperm count. Balancing the hormonal functions, the rose encourages a regular menstrual cycle and eases painful periods. Rose is a soothing remedy for emotional difficulties around the menopause. For women who feel insecure about their sexuality and lack confidence in loving, intimate relationships, this remedy also offers much help.

Rose calms and nurtures, soothing anger and irritability; it comforts and helps to heal the wounded heart. Culpepper says it makes "a very good cordial against faintings, swoonings, weakness and trembling of the heart." Cooling, calming, stabilizing, and restoring, the rose helps us find peace within; we have much need of its love and generous spirit.

GUI PI TANG

resolve the spleen decoction

This is a formula that is both strengthening and calming. In Chinese medicine the spleen (Earth) is related to the digestion and "generates blood." When the spleen is weak the blood has a deficient quality, and does not nourish the heart or hold the spirit. We become prone to anxiety, apprehension, insomnia, palpitations, and withdrawal. We also lose our ability to concentrate and become forgetful and absentminded.

The chief herbs of this formula strengthen the digestion, allowing all the goodness from the food we eat to nourish us. These are *ren shen, huang qi, bai zhu*, and *zhi gan cao*. *Long yan rou* and *dang gui* help to "root" our spirit by tonifying the blood and calming our spirits. *Suan zao ren* and *fu ling* support this with their relaxing qualities. *Zhi yuan zhi* calms the spirit by moving these herbs through the heart. *Mu xiang* helps us to digest this.

Sheng jiang and *da zao* help to stengthen the protective and nutritive *qi*, aiding the beneficial actions of the other herbs.

Tonify the Spleen Decoction is strengthening to the earth element and the digestion. It is called for if there is a pale complexion, weakness, and lack of appetite. This, and the next decoction, give us the strength to accept ourself and let go of what we no longer need to carry.

11

Radix ginseng (ren shen)
Radix astragali membranacei
  (huang qi)
Rhizoma atractylodis
  macrocephalae (bai zhu)
Sclerotium poriae cocos (fu ling)
Semen zizyphi spinosae (suan
  zao ren)
Arillus euphoriae longanae (long
  yan rou)
Radix aucklandiae lappae (mu
  xiang)
Honey-fried Radix glycyrrhizae
  uralensis (zhi gan cao)
Radix angelicae sinensis (dang
  gui)
Honey-fried Radix polygalae
  tenuifoliae (zhi yuan zhi)
Rhizoma zingiberis officinalis
  recens (sheng jiang)
Fructus zizyphi jujubae (da zao)

TIAN WANG BU

emperor of heaven's special pill to tonify the heart

XIN DAN

Radix rehmanniae
glutinosae (sheng di
huang)
Radix salviae miltiorrhizae
(dan shen)
Radix angelicae sinensis
(dang gui)
Semen biotae orientalis (bai
zi ren)
Radix polygalae tenuifoliae
(yuan zhi)
Sclerotium poriae cocos (fu
ling)
Radix ginseng
(ren shen)
Tuber asparagi
cochinchinensis
(tian men dong)
Tuber ophiopogonis
japonici
(mai men dong)
Radix scrophulariae
ningpoensis (xuan shen)
Fructus schisandrae
chinensis (wu wei zi)
Semen zizyphi spinosae
(suan zao ren)
Radix platycodi grandiflori
(jie geng)

This Chinese herbal formula is said to have come in a dream from the

emperor of heaven. It is a classic formula that is used to enrich the *yin*,

nourish the blood, tonify the heart and calm the spirit. In Chinese

medicine the heart holds the *shen*, which is our spirit. The heartbeat has

the role of keeping all other aspects of ourselves in order, just as a

drumbeat keeps a piece of music

together. The heart governs the blood,

stores the spirit, and it sends its fire

downward to meet the kidneys. The

kidneys store the will and essence,

which rise up to meet with the heart.

When this happens, the fire and water

within us are in balance. This formula

helps achieve this, so that our spirit

and will are both calm and settled.

The chief herb, *sheng di huang*, nourishes the *yin* and clears heat. It strengthens the kidneys (water), which helps to regulate the fire. It also nourishes the blood. The deputy herbs, *dan shen* and *dang gui*, both strengthen the blood and encourage its movement. Other deputies are *bai zi ren*, *yuan zhi*, *fu ling*, and ginseng, which calm the heart, clearing shock, and hold it steady. There are two groups of assistants: *tian men dong*, *mai men dong*, and *xuan shen*, which clear heat and nourish *yin; wu wei zi* and *suan zao ren* help to hold the heart energy within the heart. The envoy, *jie geng*, carries the prescription upward to the chest, the home of the spirit.

Emperor of Heaven's Special Pill to Tonify the Heart is used when there are symptoms of irritability, palpitations with anxiety, fatigue, insomnia with restless sleep, inability to concentrate for even short periods of time, forgetfulness, and dry stools. It may be especially helpful for women as it is useful when the fire is out of balance and there are symptoms of heat, such as a flushed face, hot flushes, and night sweats.

aesculus hippocastanum

WHITE CHESTNUT

The white flowering spikes of the chestnut tree are like candles carrying the light of peace. The essence of white chestnut helps to bring a sense of inner quiet. Dr. Bach writes, "by bringing ourselves to such an atmosphere of peace that our Souls are able to speak to us through our conscience and intuition and to guide us according to their wishes."

This remedy is especially helpful when our thoughts keep circling around in our head, and we are unable to just let go and relax. Mental arguments replay again and again as we try to come to some sort of resolution. Yet this resolution may not be discovered until we are able to stop the verbal conflict and find a place of peace within. White chestnut will find a deeper level of knowing, so that we may use our wisdom to understand what is the next step.

Physically, white chestnut treats insomnia and frontal headaches caused by an overactive mind. As we relax our thoughts, tension is released. We take a wider perspective and integrate the different aspects of our life. We remember our strengths and become less distracted by the words and judgements of others.

The aspen tree quakes and quivers with every small breath of wind, its leaves dancing in the breeze. The remedy aspen helps us overcome our trembling and fears, and the hauntings of traumatic events that are known or unknown. Some people are more vulnerable to this type of anxiety and fear. They are sensitive to atmospheres, picking up on sensations within a place or among people.

FLOWER REMEDIES

ASPEN

populus tremula

Through calming fears we come to a quieter place within ourself. In this place of stillness we come to trust that we are held by the divine power of love. A positive statement from Dr. Bach is "The development of Love brings us to the realization of Unity, of the truth that one and all of us are of the One Great Creation. The cause of all our troubles is self and separateness, and this vanishes as soon as Love and the knowledge of the great Unity become part of our nature." This remedy helps people who have become 'too opened' by certain group meditation techniques, as well as anyone who has experienced traumatic drug reactions.

CHERRY PLUM

prunus cerasifera

Cherry plum blossoms appear toward the end of the gray winter, heralding the spring. The beauty and purity of their flowers offering hope of new beginnings. Cherry plum helps us deal with fears that threaten to overthrow our good sense. Sometimes thoughts arise that undermine us and we grow desperate and fear doing something that is normally not within our nature. We may contemplate suicide or fear that we will lose control of ourself and act in a destructive way.

With every step we take there are always new possibilities. We forget this when challenged by extreme fear, and our anxiety cuts us off from our inner wisdom. Much courage is needed to move through these emotions to find a positive way forward. Dr. Bach writes about this remedy, "This drives away all the wrong ideas and gives the sufferer mental strength and confidence."

A herbalist I know wanted to give a meaningful gift to a woman who lost her husband. It was mid-winter and most of the flowers in her lovely garden were not in bloom, so she gave some home-made rose jelly. She knew that the rose carries love, warms the heart, and softens the emotions.

ROSE PETAL JELLY

recipe from *my roses*

Apples
Preserving sugar
Dried rose petals

Cut up the apples fairly small without peeling them, then put them in a preserving pan and cover with cold water. Simmer slowly to a pulp. Strain the pulp through a jelly bag and leave to drip all night into a bowl. Measure the liquid. To every pint allow a pound of preserving sugar. Stir on a low heat until the sugar is dissolved. Then put in as many dried rose petals as the liquid will hold. Boil until the jelly sets when tested on a cold plate. Strain before putting into warm sterilized jars.

HERBS
THAT
STIMULATE
AND
REVITALIZE

There are many herbs to help lift us through periods of low energy and apathy. When the struggles in our lives feel overwhelming, we may cope by becoming resigned to our difficulties, and unable to make any of the changes needed to be happy and nourish our souls' desires. We stay in the same job or relationship, but without enjoying these important aspects of life. Resignation, boredom, indifference, and hopelessness are emotions that deaden our soul and weaken our passion for living.

All things enjoy ecstatic union with nature. Life without ecstasy is not true life and not worth living.
ELIOT COWAN

HERBS THAT STIMULATE AND REVITALIZE

At these difficult times we look to herbs that invigorate and reawaken our senses. With their refreshing tastes and their volatile oils that stimulate our sense of smell, they help to clear the mind, soothe emotional turmoil, and bring a gentle sense of well-being into the body. Used through the centuries to provide courage and strength, increase memory and mental clarity, and create joy and understanding, the gifts of these healing herbs are much revered.

Many people turn to coffee, tea, chocolate, or cigarettes to give them a boost of energy. They may lift us temporarily, but if taken over a long period of time, toxins build up in the body, causing us to feel sluggish. In a negative cycle, we turn more desperately toward our addictions, craving caffeine, sugar, and nicotine to keep us going. They may get our system moving, but they offer no support to it, so we feel exhausted once we stop taking them.

Our cravings can be divided into addictions, needs, and desires. Addictions dominate our life, because we feel we cannot be happy or survive without them. The first step to letting them go is to recognize which are addictions, and which are simply needs and desires. Reducing addictions is rewarding, but also demanding and we need to be gentle and patient with ourselves, especially if there is a strong physical reaction.

It is important to know why we feel tired and weary. Sometimes we have just done too much and need a good rest. A few early nights and some restorative herbs are all that is needed in this case. More often life is less straightforward. Ongoing stresses and situations that are difficult for us to accept can be wearing both mentally and physically. We miss out on those special enriching and revitalizing moments of joy because we have become tired and jaded in our perceptions.

According to Chinese medicine there are two main reasons for tiredness. One is depletion, and is simply low energy. This may be because of lack of sleep, poor digestion, overwork, or illness. If this is the case, try taking strengthening herbs, and rearrange your schedule to get more sleep. Look at your diet and check that you are eating three meals daily. Make sure your mealtimes are not rushed and that the food you eat is of good quality. Learn to say "no" to others when they request time or

energy you cannot give, and make time for relaxation and rest.

The other reason for tiredness is a stagnation of energy, or *qi*, when it becomes "knotted and stuck," not moving in a regenerative way. We may feel tired, but also frustrated and irritable, fed up with ourselves and others. Our life seems routine and mundane, and we use the expressions "stuck in a job," "stuck at home with the kids," or "stuck in a rut." Resting will not be enough to create a change in our feelings; we need to take more positive action to get going again. Exercise helps, but we may need to make changes in other aspects of our lives as well.

For many of us, feelings of weariness and tiredness are due to both conditions. Low energy, or lack of *qi*, can lead to stagnation or lethargy. We need a certain momentum to get our energy unstuck. This is why exercise can revive a sense of alertness and vitality. Once our energy is moving, we can start to make changes that will revitalize our lives. Certain herbs are also very valuable in helping to stimulate and renew our vigor. Before using any of the herbs, check the Materia Medica (page 170) to find the most appropriate and to see if there are any contraindications.

Vervain, also called "herb of grace" or "herb sacré," has a long tradition of being used for stimulation and revitalization in the ancient rites of the Christians, Romans, and druids. It was discovered on the Mount of Calvary, where it staunched the wounds of the crucified Christ. It was used by Roman priests and priestesses to sweep and purify their altars.

WESTERN HERBS

VERVAIN

verbena officinalis

HERBS FOR THE SOUL

The druids placed vervain in water which they sprinkled on worshipers as a blessing. "Vervain was picked at the rising of the Dog Star, at the dark of the moon, just before flowering. It was taken from the earth with the sacred sickle and raised aloft in the left hand. After prayers of thanksgiving were spoken, the Druid or Druidess left a gift of honey to recompense the Earth for her loss."

Vervain is a flowering herb that grows in meadows and along roadsides, where its tiny pink flowers bring a glimpse of beauty to the traffic that rushes past. Seeing the delicacy of this plant among the tougher grasses helps us to understand the healing that it offers. Its fine, light quality is helpful in easing depression and melancholy.

Vervain strengthens the nervous system while releasing stress and tension. It is a gentle herb that acts as a nervine tonic as well as a sedative, so it is helpful with anxiety and hysteria. Because of its tonifying properties, it helps to reduce debility and exhaustion if taken over a long period of time. Combine it with St. John's wort, especially if depression or nerve pain is present, and skullcap.

An infusion of vervain cools fevers and is a general cleanser for the kidneys and liver. It is a good herb tea to drink following an illness. Use one teaspoon of the dried herb with one cup of boiling water. Steep for 10–15 minutes, then strain. Drink up to three cups a day. It can stimulate the uterus, so it is best avoided during pregnancy.

Rosemary, a much revered herb, was once used at weddings and funerals, as decoration for banqueting halls, as incense during religious ceremonies, and in magical rites. Its reputation for strengthening the memory made it an emblem of fidelity for lovers and a sacred herb of friendship. In the Middle Ages it was cultivated in the kitchen garden, and came to represent the dominant role of a woman in the house. "Where Rosemary flourished, the woman ruled," goes an old saying.

Rosemary is a tonic. Used after an illness it restores health, helping to overcome lethargy and debility. Its Latin name, *Rosmarinus*, means "dew of the sea," a reference to its refreshing effect on the spirit. It lightens depression and listlessness, reinforces the heart's desires, and is empowering – boosting confidence and faith in our potential. It warms the spirit and makes us bold.

Rosemary acts as a stimulant to the circulatory and nervous system. It directs its energy to the head, increasing the blood flow to the brain and strengthening memory and concentration. Circulation to the hands and feet is improved. Rosemary calms and tones the digestive system, especially if indigestion is due to tension and emotional upsets. A cup of warm rosemary tea is a good remedy for headaches, colds, and colic. Take care to cover the infusion during its preparation so that the steam, which contains beneficial oils, does not escape. Drink up to 8 fl oz (227 ml) of tea daily. Do not use if you have a history of high blood pressure. Use with caution during pregnancy. For a warming and stimulating bath, add rosemary twigs or oil to the water. This is an excellent 'pick-me-up' after a tiring day to ease aching muscles.

Oil of rosemary is stimulating to the hair follicles and, massaged into the scalp, may prevent premature baldness. Rosemary is found in shampoos and conditioners for this reason, as well as for its cleansing properties. A hair rinse can be made from a pot of rosemary tea. For shining hair, pour a cooled infusion of tea over the hair after washing it.

Thyme, or *Thymus*, is derived from the Greek *thymon*, meaning courage. In ancient times this plant was used to invigorate and inspire courage. Roman soldiers used to bathe in thyme water to restore their vigor and strength. It is also said that a thyme bath will help to wash away the sorrows of the past.

WESTERN HERBS

THYME

thymus vulgaris

Thyme is a powerful antiseptic and preservative. The ancient Egyptians used it for embalming, and it is still one of the ingredients used for preserving specimens. To purify a room, put a few drops of thyme oil in a small bowl of steaming water. Alternatively, make a pot of thyme tea and use it to wash surfaces.

The heady scent of thyme remains in a room long after the herb is gone, overpowering and cutting through other smells, reminding us of steadfastness and sweetness. It inspires us to find courage to face the struggles we encounter each day. Beneficial to depressive states characterized by withdrawal, pessimism, and self-doubt, thyme encourages the soul with its warmth and vigor. It restores morale and spiritual fortitude by helping to overcome feelings such as fear, apathy, and a lack of confidence.

Medicinally, thyme is useful for ongoing catarrhal conditions such as coughs, colds, and sore throats. Infuse the herb in a pot of boiling water to make a tea and sweeten with honey. Add a sachet of thyme to the bath as an excellent treatment for whooping cough or a convulsive cough. Stimulating to the digestion, thyme encourages appetite, eases bloating, and relieves flatulence. It is also a useful cure for hangovers.

Peppermint has always been a popular herb. It was used by the ancient Egyptians, Chinese, and Japanese for cooking, medicines, and perfumes. The Greeks and Romans scented their bath water with it, and wove it into crowns for religious ceremonies. It was thought to stimulate clear thoughts, concentration, and inspiration.

Peppermint is an excellent herb for the digestion. It relaxes the muscles, is antiflatulent, and stimulates digestive juices. The volatile oil acts as a mild anesthetic to the stomach lining, allaying feelings of nausea.

The antiseptic qualities of peppermint make it a useful gargle for sore throats. It is also an excellent cold remedy, helping to open the skin pores and cause sweats. Hot peppermint tea warms and wards off the colds and flu of winter. It is a good inhalant to clear catarrh and blocked sinuses.

Reviving and refreshing, peppermint clears our palate and stimulates our senses. It helps keep the mind alert and clear and is very gentle, so it can be drunk by everyone, including children.

27

Chen pi is the Chinese herbal name for tangerine or citrus peel. It is used to improve digestion, and to relieve symptoms of bloating, belching, fullness, and distension. In Chinese herbal formulas it is often used with many of the more tonifying herbs to prevent stagnation, because many tonic herbs are cloying in their nature. It makes the tonifying herbs more digestible and helps our body assimilate their goodness. The sharp, tangy taste of the citrus peel refreshes and invigorates. Maybe this is the reason why we enjoy marmalade so much on our toast in the mornings.

GINSENG AND

radix ginseng and granum floris pollinis

BEE POLLEN

Ginseng is a very valuable and prized Chinese herb. An excellent tonic for the *qi*, or energy, it is strengthening and supporting for the digestion and lungs. Calming and steadying to the heart, it eases anxiety and insomnia. Its nature is *yang*, and slightly warm. Taken with bee pollen, the *yang* of the ginseng is balanced by the *yin* of the bee pollen. Bee pollen is *yin* in nature and so is nourishing and restoring. It lifts the spirits, and relieves palpitations and insomnia. By enhancing immunity it increases our resistance to infections and allergies, particularly hay fever. Both herbs are reputed to promote longevity. Together they complement one another, creating a tonic that is strong but balanced.

Six Gentlemen's Decoction is an effective remedy for tiredness, loss of appetite, nausea, loose stools, weakness in the limbs, low, or soft voice. It is not necessary to have all these symptoms for it to be of benefit, but tiredness is an important indication. This remedy also reduces catarrh, so it can ease tight-chestedness and clear copious phlegm. It is a good remedy to take after a cold or flu that fails to clear completely, especially if tiredness and catarrh linger.

CHINESE HERBS

SIX GENTLEMEN'S

liu jun zi tang

DECOCTION

The first four herbs in the Six Gentlemen's Decoction come from a formula to tonify *qi*, or energy, called the Four Gentlemen's Decoction. Ginseng is strengthening and calming. *Bai zhu* and *fu ling* are supportive to the digestive system, encouraging appetite and absorption of the nutrients from our food into the blood stream. *Zhi gan cao* takes the benefits of this prescription to all parts of the body. The last two herbs in the decoction are *chen pi* (see page 28) and *ban xia*. *Ban xia* encourages a downward movement in the digestion so it helps ease feelings of nausea. This prescription contains herbs that are both strengthening and moving.

Radix ginseng (ren shen)
Rhizoma atractylodis macrocephalae (bai zhu)
Sclerotium poriae cocos (fu ling)
Honey-fried Radix glycyrrhizae uralensis (zhi gan cao)
Pericarpium citri reticulatae (chen pi)
Rhizoma pinelliae ternatae (ban xia)

This remedy is beneficial when tiredness is due to a chronic disease, or loss of blood, such as after childbirth or a heavy period. It is also appropriate for symptoms such as palpitations with anxiety, reduced appetite, tiredness, light-headedness, and vertigo. By strengthening the *qi* and nourishing the blood, it enables us to become stronger and steadier.

Radix ginseng (ren shen)
Rhizoma atractylodis
    macrocephalae (bai zhu)
Sclerotium poriae cocos
    (fu ling)
Honey-fried Radix
    glycyrrhizae uralensis (zhi
    gan cao)
Radix rehmanniae
    glutinosae conquitae
    (shu di huang)
Radix paeoniae lactiflorae
    (bai shao)
Radix angelicae sinensis
    (dang gui)
Radix ligustici chuanxiong
    (chuan xiong)

WOMEN'S

ba zhen wan

PRECIOUS PILLS

This ancient Chinese formula tonifies *qi* and nourishes blood. It is particularly useful for women. There are four strengthening herbs that work with the *qi* and four nourishing herbs for the blood. The herbs for the *qi* are those of the Four Gentlemen's Decoction – ginseng, *bai zhu*, *fu ling*, and *zhi gan cao*. *Shu di huang* enriches the blood, as well as d*ang gui* and *bai shao*. *Chuan xiong* works with the blood to encourage circulation. These eight herbs, also known as Eight Treasures, help to anchor our spirit in everything we do.

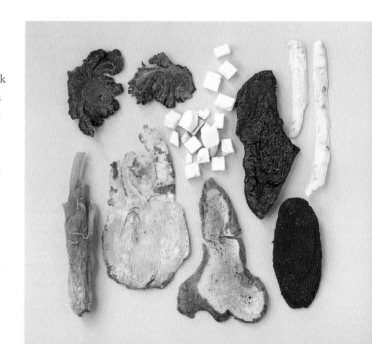

WILD ROSE

rosa canina

This flower remedy is taken from the dog rose, the ancestor of many cultivated roses. It grows in the hedgerows with its flowers facing the sun – five pink heart-shaped petals around a golden center. Like the flower itself, contemplation of this remedy helps us to rediscover our love of life and open ourself to its joy and warmth.

At times we may find ourselves facing many struggles, and cope by becoming resigned to our difficulties, feeling unable to make any of the changes needed to create a happier life. We may stay in the same job, relationship, or home, even though we do not want to be there. Boredom, resignation, hopeless, sadness, indifference, and apathy are all indications that this is the remedy that is needed. Wild rose helps to revive our vitality and interest in life so that we can live with a spirit of joy and adventure.

HORNBEAM

carpinus betulus

The hornbeam is a sturdy and adaptable tree, able to grow in many conditions of soil and weather. A hard wood, it was traditionally used to make mallets, cartwheels, and yokes for oxen, and its logs were a good source of fuel. It supports us, helping us to accomplish our ambitions, as well as simple everyday tasks.

The flower remedy hornbeam is useful for the tiredness that is often associated with the more everyday aspects of life. We may feel dull or heavy-headed at work or school, but when invited to do something we enjoy, such as going to the cinema, we feel fine. The thought of the many tasks we need to do looms like a dark cloud, making us feel weary. Procrastination is a good indication that this remedy is appropriate.

ROSEMARY WINE

White wine with rosemary acts as a tonic for circulation and nerves.

1–2 sprigs of fresh rosemary
1 bottle of white wine, preferably organic

Finely chop one or two good quality twigs of rosemary and pour a bottle of white wine on top of them. Strain off after a few days and rebottle. Enjoy a glass a day to help ease palpitations or headaches, and revitalize the circulation. Store and drink at room temperature to enhance the warming effect of rosemary.

HERBS
THAT
STRENGTHEN
AND
FORTIFY

At certain times in our lives we all may find ourselves in a state of nervous or physical exhaustion. Whether this is due to overwork, long-term illness or an ongoing stressful situation, we need help to restore equilibrium. Exhaustion is the body's way of letting us know that we need to make some changes. By listening to the soul, we can feel the way forward and start the process of rebuilding our health. Changing our work circumstances or taking a restful vacation might be a start. Acupuncture, nutritional therapies, massage, and other complementary therapies can also help. So, too, can the many revitalizing herbal treatments that strengthen us and rebuild our reserves.

HERBS THAT STRENGTHEN AND FORTIFY

Debilitating illnesses, such as shingles, ME, and rheumatism, may result in low spirits and physical weakness. Colds and flus may leave behind phlegm that is difficult to clear. Gastric viruses can weaken the digestion, so that we are prone to bloating and bowel complaints. It is important to make sure we completely recover from illness. Taking a herbal tonic will nourish and tone the body, aiding total recovery.

Adrenaline is a hormone the body uses to activate us in an emergency.

Extra stress and strain affect the adrenal medulla, the site where adrenaline is produced. This hormone is responsible for our "fight or flight" response, when our breathing is stimulated and our blood pressure, pulse rate, and heart output are raised. Sugars are released into the blood stream and the blood supply is directed toward the muscles.

After a period of long-term stress our body begins to react like this even when the circumstances that caused the stress come to an end. There may be no cause for panic and palpitations, but these symptoms will still feel very real. This can be exhausting for the system, and lead to general debility and weakness. Herbs are a powerful way of rebalancing hormonal activity and replenishing ourselves.

Long-term drug use, either recreational or medicinal, can also weaken the body, especially the liver and kidneys. For example, steroid treatment, often used for asthma and arthritis, puts strain on the adrenal glands and unbalances the production of our own natural steroids. Many of these medications can be lifesaving, but they may have harsh side effects. It is important to obtain professional medical advice about coming off or reducing these medications, and how to do it safely. Herbs can be taken alongside medication to moderate the side effects of drugs, but seek help from a qualified herbalist. In addition to taking herbal treatments, the following practical suggestions will help to strengthen and fortify us.

A good night's sleep is a wonderful way to recover from overwork, illness, or ongoing stress. While peacefully asleep the body, mind, and spirit can repair and restore themselves. To benefit most from sleep, it may be necessary to prepare for bedtime. A warm bath, with lavender or chamomile, for instance, can

Where the sunshine of joy and love can warm us, the seeds of new life will germinate, and if we allow them to grow, the herbs of the field can flower for our healing.
JULIAN BARNARD

be very soothing and relaxing. Doing some gentle stretching exercises that release muscle tension also encourages deeper relaxation during sleep.

Diet is vitally important in making a strong recovery from an illness or a state of exhaustion. By eating healthy foods at regular mealtimes, we can replenish the vitamins and minerals that are the building blocks of the body. It is best to eat three meals a day, avoiding skipping meals and "lunches on the run." Mealtimes should include time for digesting foods. Eating fresh fruit and vegetables and avoiding processed foods and sugars will really make a difference to the strength of our energy.

Taking daily exercise has several benefits. It tones our muscles and makes us feel good about our bodies. It moves our *qi*, or energy, encouraging better digestion of our food, and a stronger circulation of the blood. It also encourages us to breathe deeper, clearing our lungs and revitalizing our blood with fresh oxygen. Finally, it releases stress, tension, and frustrations. Hopefully it will be fun, too.

NETTLES

urtica dioica

The nettle is known by many for its irritating sting, so its gifts are often ignored. Organic gardeners, however, are reclaiming the value of the nutrients it contains, using it as a fertilizer for the soil. British herbal tradition has much to say about the nettle, and so it should as the nettle has much to offer. Culpepper writes, "It is under the dominion of Mars. Mars is hot and dry, and winter is cold and moist: that is why nettle tops eaten in the spring consume the phlegmatic superfluities in the body of man, that the coldness of winter has left behind."

Nettles strengthen and support the whole body. They contain iron; magnesium; potassium; trace minerals of silicon, phosphorus, chlorine, sodium, and sulfur; and are rich in vitamin C. Nourishing for the blood, they are also good for the circulation. Symptoms of weakness, tiredness, dizziness, and pale complexion, all of which are found in anemia, can be helped by drinking nettle tea. Nettles are also astringent in nature, so they stop bleeding, either internally or externally. Heavy periods or frequent nose bleeds will be lessened by taking this herb. Culpepper suggests putting a bruised leaf or seed up your nostril to help with the latter – something I have not tried!

Nettles are also diuretics and detoxifiers; they support the liver and kidney functions. General body or ankle swelling and puffy eyes in the morning may be due to the congestion of fluid in the body. Tiredness, skin problems, and urinary infections can indicate that the kidney's function of purifying and releasing fluids is under strain. Aches in the joints, weariness, and irritability can also be symptoms of a build-up of toxicity (see chapter

five). Sometimes, when we are low, we need to use herbs to boost the body and clear toxicity, and nettle is an excellent choice.

Nettle tea is a good, safe tea to drink. Add honey if you prefer it slightly sweeter. It has a mild flavor and is very nourishing, especially as a blood tonic for women. Nettles can also be used in cooking, but pick the new tops in the spring. It makes a delicious green soup, which can be frozen and then eaten in the winter months. Nettle is a herb that knows about surviving, being able to grow almost anywhere, and using a vicious sting to protect itself. Yet it is most gentle with the butterflies who love the nettle.

Oats, oat berry, straw, or oatmeal are all names of a food and medicine that helps to build and strengthen the body. Oats help to overcome symptoms of fatigue, weakness, low immunity, nervous exhaustion, poor memory, and forgetfulness. They contain trace minerals of silica, phosphorus, magnesium, calcium, iron, and potassium, and so help to build the body from the inside out.

WESTERN HERBS

OATS

avena sativa

The hearty, warm taste of oats is especially supportive to the nervous system. Combined with other remedies as a food or herbal tincture, oats are a safe addition that can be used over long periods of time and in chronic conditions. In a herbal combination they fight symptoms that arise from drug withdrawal. They dissipate feelings of light-headedness, help us to relax, and gently encourage sleep.

Oats are soothing to the digestive system, helping to restore the acid/alkaline balance in the stomach, and easing indigestion and heartburn.

Oats are a particularly safe, gentle remedy for children and will build them up after a long illness. Added to a prescription of herbs as a general strengthener, it helps children who suffer with asthma and are prone to colds. I've used it as a remedy for children who have been through periods of stress in the home, such as divorce, and may have developed problems sleeping or other complaints. Children troubled by phobias, such as fear of the dark or of school, may be supported by this remedy. Oats help to restore stability within all of us.

This tall, reedy plant, topped with feathery catkins that resemble a horse's tail, is a builder and regenerator of bones and tissues because of its high calcium and silica content. It is a remedy that breaks down the most hardened deposits within our system, and is a successful treatment for arthritis, gout, cysts, arteriosclerosis, and urinary stones. At the same time, it helps to regulate the mineral balance within the body and thus enriches our blood and nourishes us.

WESTERN HERBS

HORSETAIL

equisetum arvense

The herb strengthens the urinary system, helping to restore kidney function and stop leakage from the bladder. Horsetail also promotes urination and the cleansing of the body through the kidney function, helping to relieve symptoms of water retention, cellulite, sweating, and kidney stones. It can be taken safely over a long period of time, but is best combined with other herbs to tonify or detoxify the body.

Borage has a long tradition as a herbal remedy. Its recent resurgence is due, in part, to the beneficial support it offers when taken with medical drugs. This herb has a restorative effect on the adrenal glands, reviving and renewing their functions after the use of steroid and cortisone treatments. As these treatments become more popular, the healing gifts of borage are being rediscovered.

Like the nettle, borage is largely found growing wild on wastelands and trash heaps. It used to be grown in kitchen gardens, where it was much valued as a herb and for its flowers, which are the source of an excellent honey. It has green, furry leaves and bright blue flowers. Grieves observed in 1931,"Our great grandmothers preserved the flowers and candied them."

Gerard continues on the virtues of borage,"Those of our time do use the flowers in sallads to exhilarate and make the mind glad. There be also many things made of these used everywhere for the comfort of the heart, for the driving away of sorrow and increasing the joy of the minde. The leaves and floures of Borage put into wine make men and women glad and merry and drive away all sadnesse, dullnesse and melancholy, as Dioscorides and Pliny affirme. Syrup made of the floures of Borage comforteth the heart, purgeth melancholy and quieteth the phrenticke and lunaticke person. The leaves eaten raw in gender good bloud, especially in those that have been lately sick."

Although there is little modern scientific evidence, past traditions talk of borage as one of the four heart tonics, along with violet leaf, rose petal, and sweet woodruff. As Mattiolli recorded in 1611, "It strengthens the heart and Vital Spirit, takes away anxiety, depression and grief." It is our loss if we choose to ignore centuries of experience and forsake the gifts of this herb. My favorite saying about borage is "Borage brings courage." It can grow outside my back door any day, and I will pick a few tender leaves in the spring to add to my teapot.

LICORICE

glycyrrhiza glabra

Licorice root is a sweet herb, and its distinct flavor is known and loved by many people. Records of its medicinal use date back to the ancient Greeks in the third century B.C. Popular among the Romans and cultivated by medieval Europeans, especially those in warmer climates, it made its way into their apothecaries.

The sweet nature of licorice is strengthening and soothing to the digestion. It helps with the absorption of minerals and soothes the digestive discomforts of heartburn and mild constipation. It combines well with other herbs. Wild oats, nettle, and licorice, for instance, builds up a reserve of strength and helps overcome fatigue and debility.

Western research has shown this herb's talents at strengthening and stimulating the immune system through its effect on the pituitary and adrenal glands. To tonify the adrenal glands after using steroids, take a small daily dose of the tincture over a long period of time.

Licorice's soothing and moistening qualities are traditionally used to treat dry coughs and tight chests, combining well with other herbs to treat these symptoms. It calms inflammations and irritations in the body, mind, and spirit. It allows those emotions that are difficult to express to be released more gently. It is a gem of a herb, offering generous healing for many conditions.

Gou qi zi, Chinese wolfberry, or lycium fruit, is a small, bright orange berry. It has a sweet taste and is nourishing for the blood and *yin*. A gentle herb, it helps to replenish us. Tiredness caused by a long-term illness or aging will gradually ease. Dizziness, tinnitus, weakness, and dryness due to depletion may be helped by *gou qi zi*. Combined with Chinese licorice (*gan cao*), it makes a balanced tonic for menopausal women, treating fatigue and dryness. According to Chinese medicine, as we age the *yin* aspects of ourselves decline. *Gou qi zi* restores the *yin*, giving our skin and muscles more elasticity and suppleness.

According to folk medicine, 10 grams of this herb should be steamed and taken two to three times a day for diabetes. It also can be baked into breads and puddings. Many Chinese supermarkets sell it in cartons as a drink, or as granules to make a tea.

GINSENG

radix ginseng

Considered to be a herb that increases longevity, ginseng is one of the most precious and valued herbs in Chinese medicine. Translated from the Chinese ideogram, ginseng means "essence of the earth in the form of a man," or "man-root," because the root is said to resemble the human form. Ginseng is known as a "cure-all," a tonic for the whole body, energizing and restoring our *qi*.

Ginseng is an excellent remedy for extreme collapse, shock, or loss of blood. Chronic conditions of depletion, with symptoms such as shortness of breath, wheezing, lack of appetite, diarrhea, and prolapses are helped, regardless of whether these are due to a serious illness, long-term stress, or aging. It works as an immune enhancer, increasing the production of white blood cells to fight viruses. With the digestion, it lowers blood sugar (helpful for diabetes), improves appetite, and reduces harmful cholesterol. It stimulates sexual functions for men and women, and increases sperm count. Take it on a short-term basis for three to four months, or as a rejuvenating tonic.

According to Chinese medicine ginseng supports the heart *qi* and calms the spirit. The heart holds our true spirit; like a drum it beats a rhythm for the rest of the body to follow and become at peace. Ginseng benefits the heart *qi* by supporting us, so we are less vulnerable to the ups and downs of life. When we feel we can cope, our spirit is calm and undisturbed by what life brings. According to scientific studies, ginseng helps us to cope with stress and anxiety. It is an adaptogen, calming tensions or reviving us when

tired, depending on what is needed. Protecting against the harmful effects of stress, it strengthens us physically, emotionally, and mentally.

There are many types of ginseng root, some which are cultivated. The "wild mountain root" grows in the mountainous forests of northern China, and is considered the best quality. Cultivated root, which is prepared by steaming, is called red root (*hong shen*) and is warmer in nature. Most of the Korean ginseng is of the red variety. American ginseng (*Radix panacis quinquefolii*), grown in the mountains of Canada, is more tranquilizing and cooling, and is very beneficial for recovery from a high fever. Do not use ginseng if you are not feeling depleted or weak, or if you have high blood pressure. Avoid this herb if you are pregnant.

BU ZHONG

tonify the middle and augment the *qi* decoction

YI QI TANG

This is a basic formula that is often modified to treat different conditions. I have used it to treat various conditions, from digestive complaints to depression. It is a good remedy for muscular complaints, and is helpful for conditions that are "off and on" (and often worse with tiredness). Because of its lifting energy, this formula helps with low spirits, and those times when we want to curl up and hide away.

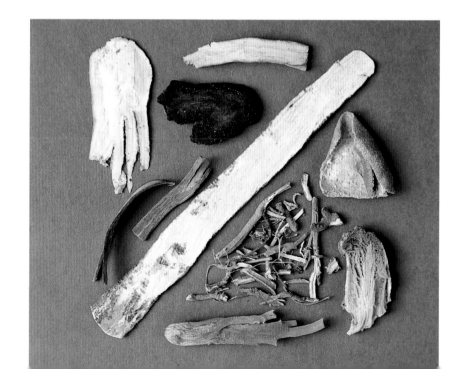

The chief herb is *huang qi* and this strengthens and raises the *yang qi* of the stomach and spleen. Combining this with *ren shen*, *bai zhu*, and *zhi gan cao* creates a tonic for the earth element, similar to the Six Gentlemen's Decoction (see page 29). The *dang gui* is an assistant herb that nourishes and moves the blood. *Chen pi*, another assistant herb, helps to make this formula more digestible, which is especially important if this is a weakness within the body. There are two envoy herbs, *chai hu* and *sheng ma* that help to raise the the sunken *yang qi*, supporting the action of the chief herb *huang qi*.

This formula is a tonic for the spleen and stomach *qi*, or energy. Both belong to the earth element, and relate to our digestion. The stomach *qi* breaks down our food, and the spleen *qi* helps with the absorption of these nutrients throughout the body. When these are weak, our muscles and limbs are not nourished and weakness and fatigue set in. The middle burner (mid-abdominal area) is unable to restrain or hold things, resulting in loose stools or diarrhea. The *yang*, or rising energy, within may not develop, so we may experience a shortness of breath, especially during exertion. Our voice may be low, and speech may be difficult. We may feel the cold and desire warm drinks. With this lack of ascending *qi*, we may experience a collapsing inward, leadingto passivity and even depression. In long-term cases, prolapses may occur due to insufficient rising *qi*. The beauty of this formula is that it is not only a tonic, but also works to get our energy moving in a beneficial direction.

Radix astragali membranacei (huang qi)
Radix ginseng (ren shen)
Rhizoma atractylodis macrocephalae (bai zhu)
Honey-fried Radix glycyrrhizae uralensis (zhi gan cao)
Radix angelicae sinensis (dang gui)
Pericarpium citri reticulatae (chen pi)
Rhizoma cimicifugae (sheng ma)
Radix bupleuri (chai hu)

Gan cao, or Chinese licorice, is a versatile herb of the same botanical family as licorice. It carries many of the same healing gifts (see page 44). Tonifying to the *qi*, or energy, it helps to overcome tiredness and lassitude. Its strengthening and moistening properties alleviate coughs, especially dry ones, and wheezing.

In Chinese prescriptions, *gan cao* is often used as an envoy, or messenger, herb. It leads the prescription to all parts of the body. In addition, it moderates harshness, including the side effects of the other herbs, neutralizing some of the heat of the hot herbs, and the coldness of the cool herbs, so we are able to digest and benefit from the prescription. A diplomatic herb indeed – a perfect envoy.

Do not use this herb if you have high blood pressure as it may aggravate the condition if it is taken over a long period of time.

The olive tree is a continual giver of fruit and wood, flowering into a ripe old age, and even giving fruit in its later years. When the old trees are cut down to stumps, new growth starts to grow from the old wood. The olive is inexhaustible and this remedy brings its support to us.

OLIVE

olea europaea

The olive tree is also known as the "tree of peace." The expression "to hold out the olive branch to another" means letting go of the struggle with other people and within ourself. In this place of letting go and finding peace we begin to experience healing and restoration.

This remedy is for those depleted after a long struggle with illness or life events. It is also for those who have given much to others and have little left for themselves. My experience of this remedy is that it brings us back to why we are here and to what is truly important in our life. When we are tired and must use the little energy we have wisely, it helps us to say "no" to anything that distracts us from nourishing ourselves. Its affirmation is, "We each have a Divine mission in this world, and our souls use our minds and bodies as instruments to do this work, so that when all three are working in unison the result is perfect health and perfect happiness."

The English oak is the sacred tree of the druids. It is sturdy and strong, a wood that has been used in the building of cathedrals and great ships. The oak plays host to numerous insects and birds. Its open branches let the light filter down so that new growth can take place beneath. It is abundant with its acorn seeds, providing food for animals and people.

OAK

quercus robur

This description of the oak tree gives us a picture of the people who may need this remedy. Their strength and giving nature may be undermined by their inability to know how to accept their limitations. Instead, they struggle on, uncomplaining until they eventually break down. This remedy is for those who are usually strong, but may be experiencing illness.

Its affirmation is, "Our whole object is to realise our faults, and endeavour so to develop the opposing virtue that the faults will disappear from us like snow melts in the sunshine. Don't fight your worries, don't struggle with your disease, don't grapple with your infirmities: rather forget them in concentrating on the development of the virtue you require."

There are a good many varieties of ginseng, differentiated by where they are grown and how they are prepared. The best quality is wild and comes from the Jilin Province in China. A good piece of ginseng root is thick and long with a thin outer skin. White ginseng is a pale yellow color, while the red ginseng (cured by steaming) is reddish-brown and translucent.

GINSENG BRANDY

This is a strengthening and warming tonic that goes down a treat!

Herbalist Michael McIntyre, who gave me this recipe, quotes from the *Shen Nong Ben Cao*, written in the 1st century A.D. about ginseng "tonic to the five viscera, quieting the spirits, fortifying the soul, allaying fear, expelling evil effluvia, brightening the eyes, opening the heart, benefiting the understanding and, if taken long enough, invigorating the body and prolonging life."

Ginseng is a very beneficial herb when taken in the appropriate circumstances (see page 45). Please refer to the Materia Medica (see page 183) before taking this herb. Do not use it if you are pregnant or if you have high blood pressure.

4 oz (100 g) good-quality ginseng root
1¾ pt (1 liter) of brandy

Chop the ginseng into large pieces that fit into the brandy bottle. Drop into the brandy, and let it sit for two to three weeks in a dark cupboard. Drink one teaspoon, or 6 ml, a day to help restore vitality and strength. Avoid using ginseng if you have high blood pressure, or during pregnancy.

HERBS

THAT

GLADDEN

THE HEART

Courage and a warm heart are virtues that bring joy and meaning into our lives. Feeling loved, and taking the risk of loving someone else, are courageous acts that require us to face the fear of rejection and loss. Developing a warm heart and a generous spirit, and being there for another, strengthen us and feed the soul.

HERBS THAT GLADDEN THE HEART

Each of us reacts in our own way to life. Any experience, whether difficult or joyful, provides us with an opportunity to express who we are through our choice of actions and words. In this way we define who we are, show our wisdom, or perhaps ignorance, and begin to find out more about our soul.

Life's challenges can be exhausting or stimulating. How we view situations and the expectations we hold for ourselves and others often determines our reaction. We may feel we can cope with certain events, only to become depressed because we did not do as well as we thought we would. Or others may not live up to our expectations and we may feel deeply disappointed. If, however, we can use every experience as a way of learning more about who we are, what is truly important to us, and what we need to change so that we can be more fulfilled and happy, then "failure" becomes an obsolete word in our vocabulary.

In our society we have created many illusions about happiness. We have conned ourselves into believing that if we have enough money, enough time, the right relationship, lover, child, or summer holiday, we would be happy. This is may be true, but for how long? And sometimes these desires are so strong that we overlook the delight in our everyday life. When we do not get what we want, we can feel depressed, ignoring all the good things we already have.

Depression can be a repression of emotions. Often, rather than express our anger, grief, or rage, we choose to become sullen and depressed.

*Full of ancient memories and mysteries, evocative
of spells and faerie tales, the hawthorne is the tree
most associated with fertility and fulfilment in the
hearts of the people, and its beautiful blossoms
were thought to help prayers reach heaven.*

JAQUELINE MEMORY PATERSON

Expressing emotions sometimes seems dangerous to us or to others, so it is safer to be depressed. Feeling hopeless about the possibility of change invites despair. In these circumstances, we need a catalyst to start a new process that will lead us out of our depression. Finding ways of bringing about a change, step-by-step, requires focus, energy, and determination. Herbs to "gladden the heart," help us to hold the inspiration, courage, and strength that is needed to have a warm heart and a meaningful life – even in difficult times.

At times depression can be a very appropriate emotion to feel, for example when we look at all the superficiality and destruction in the world. The difficulty is the negativity that depression brings. It can blind us to any real prospect of change. It prevents us from having hope, and feeling that any step toward change is possible. This can become self-reinforcing, and the more we become locked into it, the harder it is to break the cycle. It may be

necessary to get outside help, such as counselling or psychotherapy to understand the way through the depression.

The grief and sorrow caused by the loss of a loved one, or the ending of a relationship can be a lonely and painful experience. The healing of a broken heart demands tender care and love. We have forgotten how to grieve, and how to allow time for the healing of the heart and soul. Within our busy lives it often feels very difficult to take time out to rediscover ourselves. Yet, as poetry suggests, it is through experiencing pain that we come to know the richness of life and what is truly valuable and important.

The herbs listed in this chapter help to hold us steady, mend the heart, and support us while we search for joy and meaning once more.

Check in the Materia Medica (page 170) to find the most appropriate remedy and for any contraindications.

hypericum perforatum

St. John's wort is a popular herb that is widely used to relieve depression. It strengthens the nervous system and is especially helpful when exhaustion underlies the depression. Chronic depression or seasonal adjustment disorder (SAD) respond well to a regular amount of St. John's wort. Please check the cautions in the Materia Medica (see page 170) before taking this herb. Do not use it if you are taking anti-depressants or other medication. Avoid it if you are pregnant or breast-feeding. St. John's wort should not be taken by children.

According to Chinese medicine St.John's wort releases constraint, moves the *qi*, or energy, and soothes pain. Frustration, tension and depression constrict the flow of our energy. This herb encourages movement of *qi*, alleviating these states of mind. Physical symptoms of such problems can include PMS, headaches, abdominal bloating, and tight shoulder muscles. As *qi* is moved, pain and tension are released.

St. John's wort is also extremely effective if used externally in a massage oil to heal nerve pain or "deadness" in parts of the body affected by strokes and neuralgia.

Eliot Cowan, in his book *Plant Spirit Medicine*, talks about his dream of St. John's wort. This plant told him, "I will bind together what has been rent asunder." He continues, "Since that time, I have used it as cement for fractured souls."

I have followed his advice and used this herb in situations of trauma and loss, where people have been so devastated that parts of their soul seem to have gone. This may be the case in long-term depression, or listlessness. St.John's wort is a gentle healer that needs to be taken over a long period of time. It goes very deeply without fear to heal the blackness of depression.

Lavender's lilac flowers with their strong aroma help to bring us into deeper states of relaxation. In these quiet moments, we touch our souls. Tensions are eased and this spiritual state of oneness and peace can be brought back with us into everyday life.

Lavender is useful for strengthening the nerves and relieving depression. It helps to restore concentration and lift the spirits. Grieves writes, "In some cases of mental depression and delusions, oil of Lavender proves a real service, and a few drops rubbed on the temple will cure nervous headache. A tea brewed from lavender tops, made in moderate strength, is excellent to remove headache from fatigue and exhaustion...."

This remedy is also very calming and helpful with anxiety and palpitations. It eases irritability and restlessness, helps relax muscular tension, and is excellent for cramp. Use a couple of drops of lavender oil in a massage base oil and rub into the affected muscles, or have a warm bath with some lavender in it.

Lavender has a harmonizing effect on the body. It calms and comforts the mind and alleviates fears in cases of anxiety and emotional unrest. Where the problem is one of depression and depletion, it works as a stimulant, transforming depression and reviving spirits as well as consciousness.

Lavender is a gentle and practical remedy that is useful for many different situations and states of mind. Used in baths or aromatherapy burners, lavender will help create a peaceful state that brings a deep sleep. Use it with children who find sleep difficult. Make a lavender sleep pillow with dried flowers sewn into a small cotton square. It is also possible to buy lavender-scented cloth or linen. Traditionally this was used to repel insects, but it also has a sleep-inducing effect.

To aid relaxation and drain away tension, make a warm footbath and add a few drops of lavender oil. Sit quietly for 10 minutes. This will restore your spirits and relax your thoughts – your feet will feel wonderful as well.

61

LEMON BALM

melissa officinalis

Lemon balm, or melissa leaf, is a common herb that will take over the garden if given a chance. It has a wonderful lemon scent, which is released when the leaves are brushed or bruised. It was called melissa by the ancient Greeks (the same name they gave to the honey bee), and as much valued for its healing gifts as bees were for honey. *The Canon of Medicines*, written by Arabian physicians in the 11th century, describes this herb: "balm maketh the heart merry and joyful, and strengtheneth the vital spirits." Lemon balm has a long tradition of counteracting melancholy.

Lemon balm's cooling and soothing properties benefit the heart, easing restlessness, insomnia, and nervous agitation. Its moving properties help clear the "stuck" feelings that often accompany depression. Harmonizing to the soul, it gently rocks the *qi*, or energy, to move and release it. People who are emotionally sensitive are often frightened of strong emotions or confrontations and allow them to build up inside. Lemon balm will ease the intensity of these emotions, bringing serenity to the soul. As fears and intense emotions calm down, a sense of clarity and inner knowing returns.

Culpepper describes lemon balm as being under the astrological sign of Cancer. Cancer governs the breasts, pericardium, and stomach and is a symbol of our emotional roots – of mothering and childhood. Reaching deep into the psyche, the inner child of our emotional well-being, lemon balm nurtures a sense of security and peace.

As a tonifying herb, lemon balm strengthens the nervous system and our general well-being. It is a good remedy for depression following flu, or accompanying nervous exhaustion. It helps to clear fevers, as well as the restlessness and irritability that sometimes accompanies illness. By encouraging rest, it allows us to sleep and gives our body time to restore

itself. Its nourishing, healing properties help to speed recovery time after illness.

Lemon balm leaf helps to clear headaches in the temples due to tension. It is cooling and helps the energy descend downward from the head, relieving burning eyes, hot flushes, ringing in the ears, and palpitations. Lemon balm leaf tea is a good substitute for conventional coffee and tea. A gentle restorer of balance and harmony, it is a successful remedy if we are feeling pressured, rushed, overworked, red-faced, and hot.

Traditionally, meadowsweet was simmered in wine to treat fevers and to cure depression. Gerard writes, "The leaves and floures of Meadowsweet farre excelle all other strewing herbs for to decke up houses, to strawe in chambers, halls and banqueting-houses in the summertime, for the smell thereof makes the heart merrie and joyful and delighteth the senses." Its scent of honey and almonds is delightful. Use it around the house to bring in a sense of peace and cheerfulness.

WESTERN HERBS

MEADOWSWEET

filipendula ulmaria

Meadowsweet is a gentle herb that can be used safely with children, the elderly, and sensitive individuals. It contains salicylic acid, which is the basis of modern aspirin, and is useful in alleviating gout and rheumatic conditions of painful joints. It is also excellent for reducing fevers and healing the digestion. One of the best antacid remedies, it soothes heartburn, indigestion, and gastric ulcers, while relieving wind, colic and flatulence. Meadowsweet is helpful for stopping diarrhea, especially in children. It also helps to ease depression. Its relaxant properties induce a restful sleep, soothe tensions and encourage peace within.

HAWTHORN BERRIES

crataegus oxyacanthoides

The hawthorn tree, with its sweet-scented, snow-white blossoms, heralds the coming of summer. In Celtic traditions, the Beltane festival – connected with fertility and passion – was once held on the day of the first blooming of the hawthorn. Now known as May Day, it is celebrated by dancing around the maypole in the returning warmth and light of summer. The hawthorn has also been used to decorate and adorn the maypole – the symbol of fertility and the male phallus.

Medicinally, hawthorn berries are a gentle remedy for the heart and circulation. I include them here as they have a restoring and steadying effect on the heart. They help with fatigue, palpitations, and labored breathing, generally strengthening and nourishing the coronary circulation. They are also calming and soothing, helping to let go of tension and irritability, thereby making it possible to rest so that healing can take place. Their balancing nature acts to stimulate or slow the heartbeat and to steady its rhythm. This brings a sense of stability and comfort. We can open our heart and feel our passions, yet return to a secure heartbeat.

Towering linden, or lime, trees often line the walkways of city parks, their sweet scent filtering through the air. Linden blossom or tilia tea is popular in France and the honey from the flower is delicious. The tree has long associations with beauty, love, and feminine grace. The Greek for linden is Philyra, who was the mother of Chiron, the learned centaur. According to mythology, she was so ashamed of bearing such a strange offspring that she asked the gods to change her. She became the linden tree.

LINDEN FLOWER

tilia europaea

This beautiful blossom makes a fragrant tisane or tea, which is very relaxing and restoring. It eases tension and anxiety, and is an excellent remedy for fretful children. Much like chamomile with its relaxing qualities, it encourages a good night's sleep.

A remedy for the heart, it eases palpitations and chest pains, and encourages good circulation through this vital organ. It reduces high blood pressure and arteriosclerosis. It helps to dissolve hard deposits in the arteries and is an anticoagulant in the blood. Calming to the *shen*, the spirit of the heart, it soothes irritability, stress, and anxiety.

A common culinary herb, marjoram also has a long tradition of medicinal use. Its Latin name of *origanum* is derived from the Greek *oros*, meaning mountain, and *ganos*, which is joy. According to Greek mythology, Aphrodite created marjoram as a symbol of fertility, love, and honor.

Marjoram was widely used in Greek medicine and historical texts are full of comments like "strengthens the heart and quickens the bodily spirits and natural strength." The ancient Greeks used it to comfort the bereaved and planted it on graves to let the dead rest in peace.

Modern aromatherapy uses its warming strength as comfort to those who feel alone, or who have recently lost someone they love. It has a relaxing effect on both the mind and body, easing anxiety, restlessness, and internal trembling.

A useful women's herb it will relieve period pains, and delayed menstruation. Tension and anxiety, which are part of premenstrual syndrome, are also eased, along with insomnia and irritability. Some types of infertility may be treated with this herb, as it has an effect on the pituitary function.

This strongly scented herb offers warming and relaxing properties to ease tense muscles and encourage circulation. Useful for arthritic conditions, it helps to clear toxins from the joints.

MARJORAM

origanum vulgare

HERBS THAT GLADDEN THE HEART

GUI ZHI

ramulus cinnamomi cassiae

Gui zhi is known as cinnamon. This warm spice has many herbal uses in Chinese medicine. Its most obvious benefit is that it is warming and invigorating. It warms the channels and disperses cold, removing painful obstruction in joints and limbs, especially shoulders. Cinnamon also warms and moves the *qi*, or energy, through the chest, and in this way calms palpitations and releases chest pains. The smell and taste bring nourishing gifts to us, like the warmth of the sun. Perhaps this is why it is so often used in cooking through the winter celebrations.

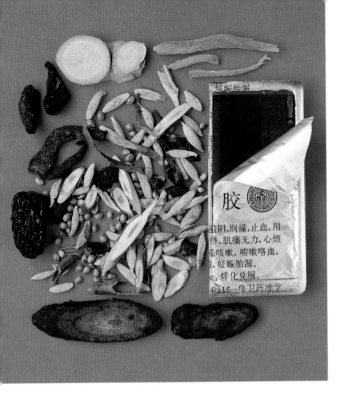

Zhi gan cao tang is a very nourishing formula – it is strengthening to the *qi*, nourishing to the blood, enriching to the *yin*, and restoring to the pulse. This strong tonic helps with symptoms of depletion, such as weakness, paleness, and shortness of breath. Palpitations, with anxiety, irritability, insomnia, and emaciation all are indications that this formula would be of benefit. It restores vitality, bringing fullness back into life.

CHINESE HERBS

ZHI GAN
honey-fried licorice decoction
CAO TANG

Zhi gan cao is the emperor herb, or the main ingredient, of this formula. Combining *zhi gan cao* with ginseng has a calming and strengthening effect, which relieves palpitations and anxiety. *Sheng di huang, mai men dong, e jiao,* and *huo ma ren* all nourish the *yin*, moistening and encouraging fluids. They nourish and build up the blood, and the fluids of our digestion.

The *gui zhi* unblocks the flow of the heart *qi*, along with the support of ginseng. The *sheng jiang* and *da zao* make the formula easier to digest. The rice wine is an important ingredient as it helps to keep the prescription moving through the body, clearing stagnation. This formula should not be used if there are any signs of diarrhea or heat.

Honey-fried Radix glycyrrhizae uralensis (zhi gan cao)
Radix ginseng (ren shen)
Ramulus cinnamomi cassiae (gui zhi)
Radix rehmanniae glutinosae (sheng di huang)
Tuber ophiopogonis japonici (mai men dong)
Gelatinum corii asini (e jiao)
Semen cannabis sativae (huo ma ren)
Rhizoma zingiberis officinalis recens (sheng jiang)
Fructus zizyphi jujubae (da zao)
Rice wine

Ban Xia Hou Po Tang is for a condition known as "plum-pit *qi*" where there is a sensation of phlegm in the throat that is difficult to clear by coughing or swallowing. A stifling sensation in the chest, often due to emotional circumstances, stops the fluids from circulating and clearing.

The chief herb of this formula is *ban xia*, which helps to move and clear phlegm, and direct the energy downward. According to Chinese medicine, phlegm can create a stifling and oppressive sensation within the body. *Huo po* and *fu ling* also work to transform the phlegm. The *sheng jiang*, or ginger, helps to nourish the digestion and stop nausea. *Zi su ye* is light, warm, and dispersing in nature.

These herbs work together to move through any obstructions that constrict or stop the movement of our energy. At the same time they help to clear the emotional blockages that may prevent us from feeling true joy in our heart.

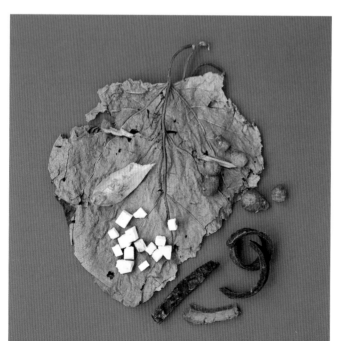

Rhizoma pinelliae ternatae (ban xia)
Cortex magnoliae officinalis (hou po)
Sclerotium poriae cocos (fu ling)
Rhizoma zingiberis officinalis recens (sheng jiang)
Folium perillae frutescentis (zi su ye)

GORSE

ulex europaeus

The brilliant golden-yellow flowers of gorse carry the strength of the sun into the new light of early spring. They are a wonderful sight after the long gray months of winter. We begin to feel the hope that comes with spring, the time of new beginnings.

Gorse is a remedy that brings renewed strength and hope to those that have suffered with long-term depression or illness. It helps us to see the light at the end of the tunnel and is an antidote to pessimism. It is useful for those who feel great hopelessness, believing that there is nothing more that can be done to change a situation. In a state of hopelessness we become more and more passive, giving up all expectation that something positive can happen. Gorse reaches deeply, like a strong ray of light, to encourage us to find hope. Its fragrance of coconut brings lightness on a sunny day.

Gentian is a small, low-growing flower that thrives on grassy, open hillsides. The young gentian plants lie flat on the earth, only growing upward in their second year. A late bloomer, the beautiful, exotic, purple flowers come at the end of summer, in September.

FLOWER REMEDIES

GENTIAN

gentiana amarella

Gentian is a remedy for doubt, pessimism, and scepticism. From its hilltop home it brings a wider vision when we become discouraged or disheartened. Bach spoke of it as people's "desire to go too much their own way, instead of seeing the bigger outlook. So the lesson of gentian is to transform our narrow doubt into understanding."

Gentian is linked to faith, not only in the religious sense, but also to a belief in the meaning of life. As a remedy, it takes us beyond our rational thoughts into a higher state of consciousness. The bright purple of its flower is the color associated with the spiritual realm.

Its late-blooming flower also teaches that our best effort is always fruitful. Each effort we make can have a positive outcome. This remedy brings the courage to overcome setbacks and delays, helping us to cope with disappointment and despondency. Bach states, "The little Gentian of our hilly pastures will help your firmness of purpose, and a happier and more hopeful outlook even when the sky is overcast. It will bring you encouragement at all times, and the understanding that there is no failure when you are doing your utmost, whatever the apparent result."

Mustard is a bright yellow flowering plant that grows freely on arable land in Britain. Flowering in spring, it brings warmth and cheerfulness with its generous colorful planting. Its prolific seedheads can lie buried for years in the earth, and when they are disturbed by plowing, new growth is germinated.

Mustard is a remedy to dispel deep gloom, especially an unexpected darkness that appears for no apparent reason. This mood can take hold quite intensely, causing physical slowness, lack of motivation, and introversion.

Of mustard, Dr. Bach wrote, "This remedy dispels gloom, and brings joy into life."

For me, the mustard seeds are tiny bursts of spice and flavor that awaken the tastebuds and warm the senses.

Sweet chestnut trees are magnificent in their height and strength. They live for thousands of years, each year bursting forth with abundant fronds of flowers in the spring and a harvest of nuts in the autumn. They are a true celebration of life with splendor.

This remedy helps release us from deepest despair. Dr Bach describes this state in *The Twelve Healers*, "For those moments which happen to some people when the anguish is so great as to seem to be unendurable. When mind or body feels as if it had borne to the uttermost limit of its endurance, and that now it must give way. When it seems there is nothing but destruction and annihilation left to face." The sweet chestnut brings its strength and exceptional life-force as a guide.

STAR OF
ornithogalum umbellatum
BETHLEHEM

The Star of Bethlehem is a delicate, white, six-pointed flower that thrives in fields and grasslands. Growing in the fields of Palestine and Syria, it has a strong association with the Star of David. This symbol holds the three aspects of the divine world touching the earth, merging with the material world reaching toward God.

Star of Bethlehem is for shock. When we suffer shock we have a tendency to separate from our body and lose contact with our soul. This flower's strength and radiant purity helps to bring us back, so that healing can be assimilated into all aspects of our being. It reunites the divine with our physical body, helping us to find peace.

NERVE TONIC OIL

This beautiful red massage oil is excellent for healing nerve strain and pain, such as with neuralgia and repetitive strain injury. Absorbed through the skin it stimulates the healing of nerve endings, so it can be used after strokes to ease tingling and "dead" sensations.

St. John's wort flowers
Vegetable oil

Take a clean jar with a lid and fill it with flowers. Gently pour the oil into the jar until the flowers are fully covered. Close the jar and let it sit on a sunny windowsill for two to six weeks. Shake and turn the jar daily. Strain the oil through a piece of muslin into a bowl. Make sure all the plant material is removed and then squeeze all the oil out of the muslin. Label and date your preparation. Store the oil in a dark bottle away from sunlight. It can be stored indefinitely. This oil is used externally: rubbed into the affected areas several times a day. It is safe to use while taking other medications, unlike forms of St. John's wort that you take internally.

HERBS
THAT
CLEANSE
AND CLEAR

Our energy, or *qi*, needs to move freely within the body to bring healing, vitality, and a good home for the soul. If *qi* does not flow, it can become stagnant, creating toxicity. Mentally, this can cause tiredness, confusion, and a loss of motivation and excitement for life. Physically, we may feel lethargic and bloated, and experience aching joints or headaches, our eyes may look dull and our complexion may appear yellow or gray. Any of these signs may indicate that it is time for a good clear-out.

HERBS THAT CLEANSE AND CLEAR

There are a number of herbs that can cleanse our systems and restore vitality. In additional there are many useful techniques for clearing the body and mind. It is important to find the one that is best for you, as all will require some degree of discipline and changes in habits and lifestyle. It is better to start with one thing you feel capable of doing and stick to it, rather than attempt too much and give up. This only leads to frustration and further adds to our sense of negativity.

Many addictions, such as those to caffeine, sugar, tobacco, and alcohol, have both physical and emotional ties. Giving them up can mean huge changes in our life. These addictions may be related to social situations, so giving up may affect friendships and relationships with colleagues. It can be helpful to understand the positive reasons for our addictions. Does smoking help to maintain friendships with other smokers? Do we drink coffee and tea because we are really tired or out of habit? Once we understand why we do something, we can find substitutes. We are also more prepared for the feelings and emotions that may arise when we begin to let go of an addiction.

As we cleanse the body – either through a de-tox diet or the use of herbs – and leave our addictions behind we can feel very emotional. Managing these emotions will help us through the process. Physical exercise helps to get our energy moving and release our frustrations. We also feel more positive about ourselves if we are physically stronger and in better shape. Walking, jogging, dancing, yoga, and t'ai chi are just a few of many options. Choose one that suits you and fits with your daily routine.

Deep breathing and meditation enable uo to centre ourselves and promote cleansing. Taking deep lungsful of air increases the oxygen in the body. By focusing on our breathing we can slow and steady the mind. This is not done to avoid emotions, but to help us become more focused on a constructive outlet for them. We become more in control of the emotions, rather than letting them control us, and thus find a steady place inside ourselves.

Relaxation is letting go, both physically and mentally. Using breathing, gentle exercise, or music to help us relax allows the body time to heal itself. Our muscles soften and the increased blood circulation brings more nutrients and oxygen to all parts of the body. A sense of peace and well-being will give us the strength and determination to carry on. Most of us do not allow time for deep relaxation because we are constantly on call for families or work, or we have an endless list of things to do. Slowing down to be within the peace and stillness of our being, where we can listen to the wisdom of the soul, may be one of the most effective ways of changing our lives.

At times, however, we may be too low or confused to know where to begin. It is especially important to get help if you are in this situation.

Asking for help is a big step for us all. It means admitting that something is wrong. It means allowing someone else to see our problems. If you have any inkling that help might be needed, seek a qualified practitioner for their opinion on the right way forward for you. The herbs suggested in this chapter will clear the system and allow our energy to flow freely once more, restoring vitality and refreshing the soul. Before using any of the herbs, check the Materia Medica (page 170) for any contraindications.

The healing offered so abundantly and freely by the plant kingdom is indeed a greening of the human condition, pointing to the reality of a new springtime.

DAVID HOFFMANN

The dandelion is mentioned in the folklore of many traditions. There is a legend about dandelion's first appearance on earth. In ancient days when there were fairies, the first humans to arrive caused problems as they could not see these elemental beings and kept treading on them. Some of the sun loving fairies, dressed in bright yellow gowns had nowhere to hide, so they became dandelions. If you step on a dandelion it will soon spring up again, and it is said to contain the spirit of fairies.

WESTERN HERBS
DANDELION
taraxacum officinale

The common dandelion, with its bright yellow flower head, is a good tonic, as well as a cleanser. The leaves are edible and, eaten in the early spring as salad, they are a rich source of vitamins and iron. Grieve recommends "Young Dandelion leaves make delicious sandwiches, the tender leaves being laid between slices of bread and butter and sprinkled with salt. The addition of a little lemon juice and pepper varies the flavour. The leaves should always be torn to pieces, rather than cut, in order to keep their flavour."

Toxicity in the environment, as well as the tendency to drink excessive amounts of coffee and alcohol, often puts the liver under stress. When this happens, headaches, skin conditions, constipation, and fatigue can occur. Dandelion stimulates and revitalizes the liver, which is one of the main organs in the body that assists with purification. As a balancer of the digestive system, dandelion restores and protects the liver, pancreas, and spleen.

Dandelion leaves, in particular, are one of nature's best diuretics. They strengthen the kidneys and soothe irritations in the urinary system of the body, clearing water retention and promoting urination. Dandelion leaves also have the added advantage of being rich in potassium, which is sometimes leached out of the body by conventional diuretics.

The common marigold, with its bright orange petals and pale green leaves, is well-known to almost everyone. It has a strong association with the sun because it opens its petals at sunrise and closes them at sunset. There are stories of its use in the Celtic festival of Beltane, when the yellow petals, known as the "summer's bride," embodied the sun's fire and life-sustaining attributes. The flowers were woven into a garland for these May Day festivities. Its Latin name, *Calendula*, comes from *calends*, meaning the first day of every month. In the Mediterranean and Egypt where it grows, the marigold is in bloom on the first day of every month. In some traditions it is regarded as a symbol of endurance.

Marigold is a mild remedy with a wide range of actions. It clears heat and toxicity, fights infections and fungal growths, and stimulates the immune system. I combine this remedy with cleavers to help clear long-term infections in which the lymph glands are involved, as it helps to move lymphatic congestion.

It is also a good women's remedy, promoting menstruation and helping to ease period pains. In childbirth it is used to stimulate contractions and the delivery of the placenta. For this reason it should not be used during pregnancy.

Elder has a love of growing in the wild, preferring wastelands, chalky pits, and hedgerows. It will plant itself in dense shade and poor soil and still produce masses of flowers and berries. Known as the tree of regeneration, it will regrow damaged branches and root from any part of itself.

ELDER
sambucus nigra

There are many traditions surrounding the elder. Many early tribes in Britain and Scandinavia believed that the spirit of the ElderMother, who works with strong earth magic lived within this tree. The stories say that foresters would not chop down an elder without asking her permission three times over. It was often grown near English cottages to grant protection from evil influences, yet it was considered bad luck to bring it into the home.

This remarkable tree has been valued for its practical uses and medicinal gifts for thousands of years. Its wood, bark, flowers, leaves, and berries have all added much to the health and well-being of our ancestors. The name "elder" is derived from "ellar" or "kindlar" because of its hollow branches, which were blown through to kindle fire. The botanical name "sambucus" comes from the Greek musical instrument the sambuke, which is like the panpipes.

Elderflowers are known for their heady scent in the summer. When taken as a hot tea, they make an excellent remedy for the onset of colds, especially when combined with peppermint and yarrow. This will stimulate sweating and the release of toxins, helping to resolve the infection. They are a great decongestant, clearing phlegm and relieving fluid retention. Hayfever, sinusitis, and catarrhal deafness respond well to elder. As a relaxant, it soothes the nerves and calms anxiety, making it a particularly helpful remedy with irritable and restless children at the onset of an infection.

The rich purple berries are delicious and nutritious in pies and jams. They combine well with apples and blackberries. Cinnamon and other spices were often added to elderberry cordials and syrups to enhance their warming effect.

The leaves of the elder are used in creams and lotions. Their healing qualities soften and moisten dry, cracked skin. An infusion can be used as a lotion to keep away flies and mosquitoes, although this needs to be used carefully on sensitive skin. Sprains, bruises, and swollen joints benefit from the leaves being placed directly on the wounded area. Elder is also a good remedy for rheumatism, and maybe this is why there is the tradition of the elder twig being carried by farmers to prevent this condition.

CLEAVERS

galium aparine

WESTERN HERBS

As Culpepper says, "It is a good remedy in the spring, eaten (being first chopped small and boiled well) in water gruel, to cleanse the blood and strengthen the liver, thereby to keep the body in health, and fitting it for that change of season that is coming." As a liver and blood cleanser, it revitalizes the whole system, encouraging circulation and movement of energy, or *qi*. Because of its cleansing action, it is widely used in the treatment of skin conditions, especially dry types of psoriasis.

An excellent tonic for the lymphatic system, cleavers treats swollen glands, tonsillitis, and adenoid trouble. Gentle in action, it can be taken over a long period of time. It is an effective and safe remedy for children suffering the swollen glands that typically occur after chronic colds and ear infections.

This fine golden powder is a valuable herb for tonifying the mucous membranes in the body. Helpful with all catarrhal states, it clears mucus from the body and dries up its production. Golden seal is an excellent treatment for chest infections, coughs, and colds. It is a powerful tonic that is used to re-establish a balance in the digestive system after bouts of gastritis and colitis. It is an energetic herb, so it needs to be used with care and in small doses.

GOLDEN SEAL
hydrastis canadensis

Golden seal's antibacterial properties make it a useful remedy for fighting infections. Make a dilute infusion and use this as a gargle for sore throats or mouth ulcers. This herb's valuable tonic and astringent properties can stem excessive bleeding in menstruation. It moves uterine congestion, bringing relief to dragging and cramping pains. It also stimulates the involuntary muscles of the uterus, so it can be helpful during childbirth. Never use this herb during pregnancy or if you have high blood pressure.

ECHINACEA

echinacea angustifolia or purpurea

Echinacea, or purple coneflowers, are beautiful plants with tall stems and a pinky-purple, daisylike flower. In the center of the flower is a brown cone of spiky seedheads. The name comes from *echinos*, meaning hedgehog, and this prickly creature reminds us of the gifts of echinacea – it helps build up our defenses and fights infections.

A traditional medicine plant of the Native Americans, echinacea was used externally as a wound healer and internally for coughs, colds, measles, and other infections. The root was chewed to relieve toothache, and made into a local anesthetic to stop pain.

Echinacea fights both bacterial and viral infection. I find it helpful in clearing catarrhal infections, especially those of the ear, nose, and throat. Take some tincture at the beginning of colds to cool fevers and clear sore throats. Echinacea is also a blood cleanser, used both externally and internally to clear up skin infections, boils, and eczema, and promote tissue repair.

Echinacea has a very healing nature that is safe to use with both adults and children. It helps with the changes that we need to make in order to be stronger. Purifying and protecting, it fortifies the immune system.

A prominent pink flower in fields, red clover is thought to bring luck and good fortune. As a symbol of the Holy Cross with four leaves, or one of the Trinity with three leaves, it brings the blessings of the spirit.

RED CLOVER

trifolium pratense

Red clover is a blood cleanser and detoxifier, which makes it suitable for use with all types of rashes and eczema. It cleanses heavy metals and chemical toxicity, including those caused by the use of drugs. It may affect cancerous tumors, helping to dissolve them, but it is important to consult a professional. Through this cleansing, emotions may also be released and understood. It is a deep-acting remedy.

As a relaxant, it relieves stress and tension, and muscular spasm. With its moistening nature, red clover is a good remedy for dry coughs and skin conditions. In its own way it soothes and comforts, and repairs irritated tissues. Emotionally, it can bring a sense of contentment. A herb of many gifts, this gentle remedy is suited to children and the elderly.

This formula helps to ease blocked or stagnant *qi*, or energy. When blood and *qi* circulate freely, we are in good health. Bad eating habits, extremes of temperature, or emotional upsets can disrupt the normal flow of *qi*. Bloating, nausea, acid indigestion, stifling sensations in the chest, or muscle tension can indicate that this remedy may be helpful.

YUE JU WAN
escape restraint pill

Rhizoma atractylodis (cang zhu)
Radix ligustici chuanxiong (chuan xiong)
Rhizoma cyperi rotundi (xiang fu)
Fructus gardeniae jasminoidis (shan zhi zi)
Massa fermentata (shen qu)

The chief ingredient of this formula is *xiang fu*, which releases constrained *qi* and encourages it to flow freely. *Chuan xiong* works with the blood to strengthen circulation and support the movement of *qi*. *Cang zhu* helps to dry dampness and transform phlegm, both of which inhibit the easy circulation of energy. The dampness can cause tiredness, heaviness, and bloating, while the phlegm is a sticky substance that holds the energy down. The herb *shan zhi zi* works with the fires in the three burners, regulating them to ease constraint and symptoms of acid indigestion. *Shen qu* is also good for the digestion, moving food efficiently through the system, and preventing nausea, bloating, and blockages.

CRAB APPLE

malis pumila or sylvestris

This flower essence is a great cleanser, helping us transform our negativity and pettiness so that we are able to return to our true selves. At times we may carry negative thoughts or feelings. If we cannot let these go, they will become obstacles that prevent us from seeing the whole picture, or what is truly important. In either case, crab apple helps us to take a different viewpoint allowing us to feel positive.

Crab apple helps to cleanse, clear, and transform our negative thoughts and actions. It helps us come to terms with our imperfections and our humanity, granting us a greater vision of who we truly are and the meaning of our life.

Crab apple is also used to overcome traumas or nightmares, helping us to integrate and transform these experiences. This is an important remedy for sensitive people who may pick up negative impressions, such as social workers or nurses after a long night of duty. Purification happens on both the physical and mental levels. Add 10 drops of this remedy to your bath, or put four drops in a small amount of water and sip it slowly.

PINE

pinus sylvestris

Pine trees have an aromatic fragrance that is cleansing and clearing.
They grow tall, with a straight grain that makes the wood suitable for
furniture and building. This remedy helps to go to our depths to
straighten out the old knots, to comb through the tangles of our life,
to teach us that we are loved, safe, and supported.

Pine flower essence cleanses feelings of guilt, helping to release them and bring forgiveness and understanding. The guilt or blame may be due to something that happened in recent times, or may have a deep-rooted hold within. If, as children, we were not wanted or loved, we may continue to feel guilty for our very existence. We may choose to live by strict guides to right and wrong, good and evil, and never be able to live up to our own expectations. We may find it difficult to accept forgiveness and love, and to give them ourselves.

Dr. Bach writes "Health is, therefore, the true realisation of what we are: we are perfect: we are the children of God. There is no striving to gain what we have already attained. We are merely here to manifest in material form the perfection with which we have been endowed from the beginning of time."

Most people are familiar with the creamy-white blossoms of the elder tree, which are a familiar sight in summer. It has long been used for medicines and food. There are many recipes that include the flowers, leaves, or berries of this wonderful tree.

This is a well-tried and loved recipe from herbalist Christina Stapley, useful for clearing cold and flu symptoms. Its refreshing taste makes a pleasant drink in the summer, added to water or lemonade. Decorate the drink by floating a few leaves of lemon balm on top. For a warming winter drink, add to hot water with several slices of ginger root.

25–30 elderflower heads (choose perfect ones and pick when their scent is sweet)
2 kg (4lb) granulated sugar
2 lemons, sliced
75g (2 ½ oz) tartaric acid
2 litres (3 ½ pints) boiling water
ice cube bags

Put the elderflowers in a large bowl. Add the sugar, sliced lemons, and tartaric acid. Pour the boiling water on to the mixture. Stir well and cover. Stir morning and evening for three days. Strain and freeze in the ice cube bags. Use one cube with a cup of water or lemonade.

HERBS
THAT
COMFORT
AND SOOTHE

The fast pace of society encourages us to be constantly on the move. This is

exciting and stimulating if everything is going well, and our soul embraces

all that life offers. If not, frustration, impatience, and irritation can

overwhelm us, with the result that we become uncaring and judgmental

toward ourselves and others. Such stress and anxiety aggravate the

weaknesses in the body, bringing physical complications

that remind us that we may need to slow down

and take more care of ourselves.

At the end of the way
is freedom.
Till then, patience.
THE BUDDHA

HERBS THAT COMFORT
AND SOOTHE

Pressures and expectations, from both ourselves and others, affect our responses to situations. Our aspirations to look after ourselves, provide for our families, succeed at work and so on can be unexpectedly thwarted. Illness, deadlines at work, or family crises can create chaos with the best-laid plans. Demands from others can push our boundaries and we may find it difficult to say "no." We may feel frustrated by pressures that we have created for ourselves.

Certain situations can bring up emotions that are hard to cope with, such as anger, envy, fear, and frustration.

None of us escapes these feelings, and at times we get caught in them. Ignoring such emotions, or indulging and inflaming them by nursing our resentments, can make them grow. Learning to cope with them is a great skill that brings emotional wisdom, and restores happiness and well-being.

Most of us believe that we are the victims of these emotions, and that we have no control over them. If we are to transform these destructive emotions we need to recognize our role in their creation. Through meditating or closing our eyes and recalling situations where we experienced fear or anger, we notice where we feel physical tension and its effect on our body. By breathing in deeply and out slowly, we can begin to release the strain that comes with these emotions.

We may not have control over all aspects of our lives, but we can learn to become more aware of the needs of the body and mind, and in this way also satisfy the soul. Through releasing tensions from the body, and calming the mind, our soul begins to flourish with the joy of life. Our perceptions are enhanced, bringing an awareness of the beauty around us and softening the heart to its pleasure.

Relaxation exercises are an effective way to release tensions in muscles, and calm anxieties. There are many techniques, but here is one to try. Find a quiet place where you can sit or lie comfortably. Take several deep breaths, allowing any thoughts to drift out of your mind. Beginning with your toes, tense up each part of the body in turn as you breathe in, then release it as you exhale. Work upward, tensing and relaxing as you breathe in and out. Relax for five minutes after this exercise, enjoying the feeling of ease and lightness.

Warm baths are another way of releasing stress and tension. Add a strong herbal infusion to the water, using a handful of dried herbs in a pint (half a liter) of boiled water. Chamomile, lavender, and linden flower are soothing and relaxing herbs. Add a few drops of aromatherapy oils to the bath: rose to heal heartaches, orange for anxiety and nervousness, lemon balm to soothe shock and sorrow. To help relieve muscle tension, add a handful of Epsom salts to a bath that is as hot as you can stand it. It is a wonderful way of letting go of the strain of the day.

Physical touch is an important way of communicating with another person, yet its expression is often missing in our society. A hug, or a hand placed on another's arm can bring warmth and understanding at times when words fail.

Seek out a good friend who is able to listen and sympathize with your concerns. Being able to talk with someone about difficult situations can help us to shift our perspectives, and understand the situation from another viewpoint. Overwhelming tasks can be lightened with this sharing and support, as we discover we are not alone with our problems.

The herbs in this section soothe and comfort us. They combine well with other herbs that strengthen and nourish us (see chapter three) and those for cleansing and clearing (see chapter five). Other soothing herbs to consider are borage, roses, and licorice.

ALOE
aloe vera

WESTERN HERBS

This green succulent, with its thick pointed leaves, is filled with healing gel. Indigenous to east and southern Africa, it prefers temperate climates, but can be grown as a houseplant anywhere. A favorite medicinal plant of Greece, where it grows in abundance, it has been used since the fourth century B.C.

This soothing remedy relieves irritation, reduces inflammation and infection, and promotes the mending of tissue. Used externally for skin conditions such as scalds, eczema, or burns due to the sun or radiation treatment, it is very cooling and remarkably healing. Fungal infections – such as athlete's foot and dandruff – and allergic rashes respond well to aloe gel, and it is safe to use on sensitive skin and babies.

Aloe juice is used as a laxative, but it may need to be combined with ginger to stop griping pains. It enhances the digestion, encouraging the secretion of digestive enzymes, balancing stomach acid, and regulating the metabolism. Soothing and protecting to the lining of the gut, it is an effective treatment for irritable bowel syndrome, ulcers, and colitis. Do not use this remedy if you are pregnant or nursing, and avoid it during heavy periods.

This beautiful flowering plant grows in salt marshes or damp places. The medicinal properties of marshmallow, and its sister plant hollyhock, were once widely valued. Culpepper quotes the finding of the Roman naturalist Pliny, who studied herbs 2,000 years ago, "Pliny saith, that whosoever shall take a spoonful of any of the mallows, for that day be free from all threatened diseases, and it is good for falling sickness."

WESTERN HERBS

MARSHMALLOW
althaea officinalis

Marshmallow and its relative hollyhock are excellent moistening and cooling herbs. Their roots and leaves are filled with demulcent mucilage that heals gastric complaints, such as acid indigestion, heartburn, and ulcers. They soothe bladder irritation and, as diuretics, ease frequent, painful urination and help with the passing of urinary stones. Stimulating to the immune system and moistening to the lungs, they relieve dry coughs and chest infections.

This plant softens the harshest emotions, which are often reflected in physical complaints. Anger and frustration are eased through its gentleness and nurturing quality.

CHICKWEED

stellaria media

Culpepper writes, "It is a fine soft pleasing herb under the dominion of the Moon." Its name *Stellaria* comes from stellar, meaning starlike, and describes its tiny star flower. This herb, which seeds itself so prolifically in garden beds, is full of vitamins and minerals. It can be picked and eaten raw in salads, and was once considered a delicacy in Europe.

The goodness of this herb nourishes and replenishes us when we are depleted and fatigued, whether this is caused by overwork, anemia, or the malabsorption of food. Pick a strengthening combination of green herbs, such as chickweed, nettle, and dandelion from the garden and make a tea. Drink this several times a day.

As a soothing herb, chickweed can be made into an ointment or poultice and used to treat infected skin conditions such as boils or splinters. The ointment also calms rashes, eczema, piles, and burns.

As a tea, or tincture, it can be taken internally to help relieve acid indigestion, colitis, and irritable bowel syndrome. It is also an effective treatment for dry coughs, asthma, and acute bronchitis.

A traditional use for chickweed is to aid weight loss. Recent research shows that it stimulates the thyroid gland, and reduces fat cells. As a diuretic, it clears water retention. Chickweed also has a role in the treatment of arthritis, rheumatism, and skin eruptions, as it eliminates toxins from the body.

The powdered bark of slippery elm is made into a thick, white gruel or paste, then taken both as a food and a medicine. Native American herbalists used this remedy for many illnesses and were skilled at finding the appropriate barks. Excellent as a cure for dehydration and heat exhaustion, it is moistening, nourishing, and sustaining.

SLIPPERY ELM

ulmus fulva

Nowadays, slippery elm is more commonly used for digestive complaints because it is soothing to the system. Indigestion, ulcers, and gastroenteritis are helped by taking this herb. It is soothing to the guts and helps stops diarrhea. As it provides nutrients, it is useful when there is a lack of appetite or eating is difficult. Children and infants who are underweight or losing weight can be fed slippery elm, but it usually needs to be sweetened with apple juice or honey. Strengthening and sustaining, it is appropriate for use with any debility following childbirth, or chronic illness.

These tiny, scented daisy flowers are well known for their calming properties. They have become a popular plant for herb gardens or chamomile lawns, where their fragrance is unmistakable and soothing. First used in the Middle Ages for aromatic stewing herbs, it was often planted around gardens, it is believed that ailing plants will benefit from their healing properties.

CHAMOMILE

chamaemelum nobilis, matricaria chamomilla syn. recutita

Chamomile is a gentle plant that helps to relax and harmonize the energy, or *qi*. It works to balance our needs and wants, and the frustrations we feel if these are not met. When we do not get what we want, we can become more demanding of ourselves and others. Frustration and irritation can build to such an extent that, unable to see our own part in the situation, we lose our temper and blame others for the predicament. Chamomile soothes tensions and eases frustrations, resentments, and depression. Its cool, calm qualities bring us back to reality, helping us let go of our expectations, and acknowledge our limitations. Then we can accept other people's help and support.

The ancient Egyptians dedicated this herb to the sun god Ra because of its power to restore wholeness to self. It does this by offering many avenues of healing. It is first sweet to taste, then bitter, warming, yet cooling to inflammations, and calms hyperactivity. It is relaxing and yet it stimulates healing and is restoring. Through its many different aspects, it is able to balance and harmonize, soften, and moderate many different conditions. Headaches and depression, as well as toothaches, earaches, and digestive upsets, are all relieved by the therapeutic aspects of this herb. It is powerful in its gentleness.

Parkinson, in his *Earthly Paradise* (1656) writes, "Camomil is put to divers and sundry uses, both for pleasure and profit, both for the sick and the sound, in bathing to comfort and strengthen the sound and to ease pains in the diseased."

Chamomile baths are very relaxing, and good for young children before bedtime to help them sleep peacefully. Chamomile can be used externally to soothe earache, toothache, and nerve pain. To clear redness and dryness in the eyes, place some wet chamomile tea bags over your eyes, and leave for a few minutes.

This sweet, bland herb is similar in its appearance and nature to barley. It is a small, round, white seed that can be cooked and eaten as a food, as well as combined with other herbs in a decoction. A gentle herb or food, it can be used with children to strengthen their digestion and stop mild cases of diarrhea. It soothes bladder irritation and helps with urinary difficulties. Water retention, edema, and swollen joints can be treated taking *yi yi ren*, and as Bensky and Gamble say it "leaches out dampness" from the body. Use with caution during pregnancy.

YI YI REN

semen coicis lachryma-jobi

MAI MEN DONG

tuber ophiopogonis japonici

Mai men dong is a small tuberous root with a slightly bitter taste, and cool properties. Its medicinal qualities are similar to marshmallow root, so it is moistening and soothing. It nourishes dry lungs and stops coughs, it replenishes digestive juices and aids acidity and dry mouth. Moistening to the bowels, it relieves constipation. Because of its cooling nature, which strengthens the *yin*, it clears heat and calms irritability, especially when this worsens late in the day.

JU HUA

flos chrysanthemi morifolii

The chrysanthemum is a flower of contemplation and is used to decorate temple walls and sacred texts. A tea of dried chrysanthemum flowers is a traditional remedy drunk to prolong life. The tea was often used to clear the head before a period of prolonged thought. Dizziness, headache, and deafness are treated with *ju hua*. It is also a very good herb for long-standing eye conditions such as tearing, dryness, and redness. It helps to soothe irritability and calm frustrations with its cooling and harmonizing properties.

This Chinese formula helps to replenish the *yin*, or the more moistening and cooling energies of the body.

LIU WEI DI

six ingredient pill with rehmannia

HUANG WAN

*Radix rehmanniae
    glutinosae conquitae
    (shu di huang)*
*Fructus corni officinalis
    (shan zhu yu)*
*Radix dioscoreae oppositae
    (shan yao)*
*Sclerotium poriae cocos
    (fu ling)*
*Cortex moutan radicis
    (mu dan pi)*
*Rhizoma alismatis orientalis
    (ze xie)*

This formula is an elegant combination of herbs. The chief herb, *shu di huang*, nourishes the kidney *yin* and essence. This is aided by the deputies – *shan zhu yu*, which enriches the liver and stops sweating, and *shan yao*, which stabilizes the spleen or digestive energy. The assistants are more clearing herbs that prevent the tonifying herbs from becoming too clogging. *Fu ling* is paired with *shan yao* to reinforce the nourishing function of the digestive system. *Mu dan pi* drains and clears the heat held in the liver and balances the warm nature of *shan zhu yu*. *Ze xie* works with *shu di huang*, clearing heat through the kidneys, encouraging a good movement of fluids, and promoting urination.

   Liu wei di huang wan is indicated for complaints that accompany aging, overwork, or long-term stress.

   Common symptoms include weakness and soreness in back of legs and lower back, light-headedness, vertigo, irritability, hot flushes, night sweats, and insomnia. This remedy can also be very helpful for many menopausal complaints.

IMPATIENS

impatiens glandulifera

This prolific plant, with its delicate stem and unusual mauve flower, was one of the first remedies of Dr. Bach. He discovered it in the autumn, when the flower's seed pod was ripe and ready to burst. Noticing the explosive way the seeds popped out of the pod with one touch on its sensitive skin, he found the remedy for frustration and irritation. During the late summer this tall plant carries buds, flowers, and seeds simultaneously.

This remedy suits people who are fast, independent workers. Quick thinking, they may find it difficult to slow down and explain to others what they are doing. Patience may not be one of their strengths, and as a patient they will be anxious for a hasty recovery.

Dr. Bach writes of this remedy, "You are striving for exquisite gentleness and forgiveness, and that beautiful mauve flower, Impatiens, which grows along the sides of some of the Welsh streams, will, with its blessing, help you along the road."

MIMULUS

mimulus guttatus

Mimulus, or monkey flower, grows on the banks of rivers, where it

hangs over the stones and is splashed by the running waters. The bright

yellow flower, flecked with spots of red, opens wide into the sunlight

and thousands of its tiny seeds are swept into the current, lodging

among the stones to grow into beautiful, delicate flowers.

This remedy helps us conquer our known fears, such as heights, accidents, and death – the list of fears may be endless. It helps those who suffer from shyness and timidity, and find the world overwhelming. Their sensitivity and delicacy separates them from those who are more robust and able to handle a busy environment.

They may need to withdraw into their own space to recover from life, and find ways of coming to terms with their fears.

This remedy brings quiet courage and confidence. Mimulus shows us how to live with happiness and acceptance of our situation, allowing love of life to take us beyond our fears.

Enjoy a relaxing herbal bath that eases tensions away. Run a warm bath and place a muslin bag of fresh or dried chamomile under the faucet. Use 1½ oz (30 g) of fresh herbs or 1 oz (20 g) of dried herbs. Alternatively add one potful of a strong infusion of chamomile – about 1¼ pt (600 ml) to a bath. Or add several drops of the essential oil to the water. Soak in the warm water for 15–20 minutes, allowing the sweet scent of the herb to banish tensions, frustrations, and irritations through its relaxing and soothing qualities.

HERBS

FOR

CHANGES

Life is change. Movement is part of the dynamics of vitality and growth. As we quest for balance of the body, mind, and soul, change is as inevitable as the rising and setting of the sun and the cycles of the seasons. Go watch a river. Is it ever the same from one moment to another? Constantly changing and flowing, it is an inspiration for how we might travel our own "river of life." When we are at ease with change, we make the most of every situation, learning from those that challenge us. We are able to re-balance and restore ourselves, remembering who we are and the gifts we carry, and are able to share our wisdom and strength with others.

Each new step we take in life needs to be integrated within our body, mind, and soul. There is a dance that goes on between the different aspects of ourselves as we go through the process of change. Sometimes the change is brought about because of the soul's desires and we find ourself doing things that come from its prompting. We may, for instance, feel a deep longing to be with another person, or a strong desire to move home. These may not make much rational sense at the time, but are a calling from within. In these circumstances we need to understand our deeper aspirations.

At other times changes are brought on by outside circumstances, and may also be difficult or challenging. The death of a loved one, illness, moving house, and the loss of a job are all stressful experiences, and may give rise to feelings of resentment, unfairness, anger, despair, and depression. The trauma of these situations may leave us feeling that we no longer know who we are. Facing these shifts and their unfamiliar, and perhaps frightening, aspects may expose the weaknesses within ourselves.

The more we can connect with the wisdom of the soul at these times, the greater our chance of regaining balance. Our inner knowing is a guide as we move through new territory. We may also need to reach outside to friends and family for support. Counseling can help us face and express the emotions that come up at these times. Herbal remedies can assist us to find inner stillness and peace, soothing and easing the pressure.

In this chapter the focus is on herbal remedies that work with hormones. Both men and women are subject to hormonal influences that affect us emotionally and physically. For women, hormonal activity marks the key stages in our lives – puberty, pregnancy, and the menopause. Although the effects in men are less pronounced and visible, it is just as important to understand and recognize them. Adolescence and the male menopause are times when men experience changes in their bodies and emotions that often bring with them profound transformations in the circumstances of their lives. Here are some suggestions for things you can do in conjunction with the use of herbs to ease the way of change for both sexes:

Positive outlook Find the positive aspect in each moment. Through even the most difficult times we can learn something about ourselves. Feel the love of those around you. Let go of old resentments, angers, and bitterness.

Do not carry the baggage of your past into new beginnings.

Exercise Take regular exercise, starting with walking or gentle forms of yoga. Build up to more aerobic exercises, such as swimming, cycling, and jogging, but do not exhaust yourself to the point of depletion. Daily exercise keeps the energy moving, releases stress and tension, and generally makes you feel good about yourself.

Quiet time Try to keep some time for yourself. The easiest way is to set a few hours aside in your diary and say "no" to any requests if they interfere with this. Do something relaxing and allow yourself to be quiet within. Meditation, listening to music, walking in the woods, or gardening are all ways of being in a quiet space.

Workable tasks Times of change can feel overwhelming, not only because of the emotional adjustments, but also because of all the things that need to be done. Set out the positive goals you want to accomplish, and make a list of all that needs doing. Break the list down into workable tasks and do several of these each week. Do not let yourself become discouraged or distracted. Get the help and support you need to do these tasks. In this way even the most challenging changes will become manageable.

From the place of the Soul we each hold our part in the song of Creation, and from that place know who we are, why we are here, where we are going, and how to restore the Earth's harmony and balance.

ARWYN DREAMWALKER

Change can provoke such a wide variety of responses that many herbs are useful for coping with it. Stress, anxiety, tiredness, apathy, depression, or irritability are just some of the unwanted side-effects of change. In previous chapters I have discussed many of these conditions and the herbs that help to restore balance, so we are able to cope during times of transition. For example, valerian, skullcap, and passion flower will relieve symptoms of anxiety, enabling us to come to a place of stillness where we can make a decision about the next step forward.

For tiredness and apathy look to herbs that stimulate and revitalize, such as rosemary and peppermint. Both are tonics that help to rejuvenate the senses. If there is debility following an illness or period of stress, try oats, nettles, or ginseng. They are fortifying, allowing us to regain our strength and move forward with less struggle.

For the depression and melancholy that accompany difficult times, herbs such as St. John's wort and lemon balm will rebuild our nervous systems so we can cope more positively. These precious herbs offer much support to help overcome these distressing emotions. Soothing herbs such as chamomile and the Chinese chrysanthemum, *ju hua*, offer relief from irritability and frustration. Through their calming properties they help to ease us through periods of upheaval.

In addition to soothing these emotional conitions, herbs are also effective for more physical problems. For example, valerian, lemon balm, and lavender are excellent remedies for soothing headaches caused by stress. A combination of valerian, passion flower, and hops helps insomnia. Try peppermint or fennel teas to aid digestion. By using herbal remedies we can carefully begin to treat the imbalances in the body and the emotions that can result from change. The Bach Flower Remedies are a wonderful resource for supporting us through changes. They guide us to the higher parts of ourselves, enabling us to alter unhelpful patterns of behavior. Through releasing these old ways of being, they encourage us to see change in a positive light. The Flower remedies included in this chapter are suitable for men and women. Read through the Materia Medica (page 170) to get a better idea of the appropriate herbs for you.

CHANGES FOR WOMEN

Many of the herbs discussed in this chapter regulate and harmonize the menstrual cycle. Unpleasant symptoms – such as bloating, irritability, or pain – before, during or after the menstrual cycle can indicate a degree of disharmony in the reproductive system. Besides herbs, there are other ways to support a healthy menstrual cycle. Here are a few suggestions:

Diet Eat plenty of fresh fruit and vegetables. Avoid caffeine and alcohol, and instead drink herbal teas such as chamomile, lime blossom, and lemon verbena. Increase fiber and grain in your diet to avoid premenstrual constipation. Eliminate excess salt, to ease water retention.

Nutritional supplements There are several nutritional supplements that help with the menstrual cycle. Evening primrose oil, antioxidants such as vitamin E and beta-carotene, vitamin C, and a magnesium and calcium supplement can all be of benefit.

Warm soaks and massage A warm bath or massage can help relax you and relieve cramps. Add relaxing oils and herbs to the bath, such as chamomile, lavender, and rose. Make up a massage lotion by adding several drops of these oils to a base oil. Use it to rub into your feet and legs, or ask someone for a neck and shoulder massage to relieve stress and tension.

The menopause can start anytime after the age of 35 years, and may be a time of momentous change. Not only are we transforming physically, but often the menopause coincides with career moves or children leaving home. Coming to terms with this transition can be extremely difficult, but it can also allow us to rediscover our own creativity and passions, and find new fulfilment.

Menopausal discomforts, such as hot flushes, palpitations, depression, vaginal dryness, and changes in libido, can be helped by herbal medicine. There are effective herbal alternatives to HRT (hormonal replacement therapy), which do not have some of the side effects of this treatment. Combined with a careful diet, nutritional supplements, and exercise, herbs can help relieve menopausal symptoms. If symptoms are severe, it is best to consult a qualified herbalist, who will be able to prepare a mixture based on your individual needs.

Agnus castus, or chaste tree, is a popular herb for helping to regulate the menstrual system. It was well-known in the Middle Ages, when it was used in monasteries to help celibate clergy control their sexual desires. Known as "cloister pepper" and "monk's pepper" it was taken to dampen sexual drive.

CHASTE TREE

vitex agnus castus

Recent research shows that vitex agnus castus has a regulating and stimulating effect on the pituitary gland, especially in terms of its progesterone production. So it can be used to heighten sexual desires, as well as discourage them! It is used to regulate the menstrual system, normalizing hormone levels. Premenstrual tension, menopausal disorders, such as tender breasts and fatigue, and behavioral symptoms, such as low self-esteem and withdrawal tendencies, can be eased with this herb. Pour a cup of boiling water onto one teaspoon of the berries, and leave to infuse for 10-15 minutes. Drink three times a day. Alternatively, take 1-2 ml of vitex agnus castus in water first thing in the morning. To fully experience the benefits of this herb, take it daily for three months.

WILD YAM

dioscorea villosa

WESTERN HERBS

Wild yam is a well-known herbal medicine in many different traditions, from Chinese herbalism to Afro-Caribbean medicine. The Native American Meskewawi used wild yam to ease labor and afterbirth pains. It was used in early versions of the contraceptive pill.

Wild yam helps to balance the hormones, although there is still much debate among scientists about the exact nature of its effect. It works with estrogen and progesterone deficiencies, helping to harmonize the hormones through the menopause. Emotional feelings of over-sensitivity, irritability, and guilt can be linked with fluctuating hormones and this herb will help mitigate them. It will also help other gynecological conditions, such as painful and heavy periods, ovulation pains, and joint pains.

Wild yam root helps to move the qi, and relaxes spasms and tension. It is useful for a number of physical complaints such as nausea, colic, and irritable bowel syndrome. It is of great use in the treatment of rheumatoid arthritis, especially in the acute phase where there is inflammation.

LADY'S MANTLE

alchemilla vulgaris

Lady's mantle, otherwise known as "lion's foot," "bear's foot," or "dewcup," has a long tradition as a herbal remedy. Grieves writes, "The generic name Alchemilla is derived from the Arabic word, *Alkemelych* (alchemy) and was bestowed on it, according to some old writers, because of the wonder-working powers of the plant."

Lady's mantle is another herb that is very useful during menopause. It helps to increase progesterone, easing symptoms of bleeding, hot flushes, vaginal dryness, and lack of sexual interest. It is a cooling and calming herb that restores the nervous system and promotes rest. By promoting urination, it clears water retention and the sluggishness this can bring on.

The herb is effective in clearing vaginal discharges and urinary and gynecological infections, especially if it is taken with echinacea root and marigold flower. It is a good remedy for many women's complaints. Legend tells us that the leaf is the cloak of the Virgin Mary. The rainbow dew drop found within it is the miracle of the Christos.

Black cohosh is a valuable remedy handed down to us from the Native Americans. It is one of many medicinal herbs they relied on, especially for pregnancy and childbirth. Their strong relationship with Grandmother Earth guided them in their search for healing herbs and their respect for the Earth meant they lived in harmony with her, respecting the gift of her plants.

Black cohosh helps to regulate the menstrual cycle, normalizing irregular or difficult menstruation. It increases estrogen in the body, helping symptoms of premenstrual syndrome, such as irritability, insomnia, joint pains, and tender breasts. It eases menopausal complaints of dizziness, hot flushes, palpitations, headaches, and depression. It is a relaxant, so it soothes cramping pains, as well as over-sensitivity that can lead to emotional upsets.

This herb can be used in many situations where a relaxing remedy is needed. It can be very helpful for labor pains, for instance, easing anxiety and tension as well as regulating uterine contractions.

As a pain reliever and anti-inflamatory it is useful in the treatment of rheumatism and arthritis. The root works specifically with muscle and nerve pain, making black cohosh an excellent remedy for neuralgia.

Culpepper writes of this herb, "Venus owns this herb and it is under Leo. There is no better herb to drive melancholy vapours from the heart, to strengthen it and make the mind cheerful, blithe and merry. ... Besides, it makes women joyful mothers of children, and settles their wombs; therefore they call it motherwort. It allays trembling of the heart, faintings and swoonings." It is a powerful herb for the emotions.

MOTHERWORT

leonurus cardiaca

Motherwort has a strong effect on the menstrual cycle. It helps with all the symptoms of premenstrual syndrome – painful, difficult periods, tension, and irritability. Balancing and harmonizing the menstrual cycle, it works for both delayed periods and heavy bleeding. Menopausal symptoms, such as hot flushes and night sweats, can also be treated with this herb. It eases tightness in the chest and calms palpitations. In childbirth, motherwort can help with slow, difficult labor, and post-partum bleeding. It is frequently used in Chinese hospitals after delivery to help the uterus contract, reduce pain, and stop bleeding. Chinese medicine recognizes the connection to both the heart and the uterus – Motherwort offers treatment for both. It is a wonderful herb for women.

Yarrow is a versatile herb found in hedgerows and fields of wild flowers. It has heads of white small-petaled flowers and abundant feathery leaves. Its botanical name *Achillea millefolium* comes from the Greek hero Achilles, who used yarrow to heal the wounds of his friends. Yarrow is a good wound healer and was used in the First World War. It is also called "soldier's wound wort" and "staunchweed."

YARROW
achillea millefolium

As well as being a wound remedy, yarrow is good at treating gynecological disorders. It regulates the menstrual functions, from puberty to the menopause, by working with the blood, circulation, and the uterus. It helps to stem the flooding of heavy periods and to bring on delayed menstruation. Because it encourages the circulation of energy or *qi*, it helps to reduce premenstrual tension, and irritability. Varicose veins, leg cramps, and other circulatory conditions are eased by taking this herb because it vitalizes and moves the blood.

Yarrow is an effective herb for treating urinary problems, relieving irritation in the bladder, and promoting urination. Because it is an astringent, it helps with mild incontinence. It is a gentle relaxant of muscular and nervous tensions in the digestive, urinary, cardiovascular, and menstrual systems. This releasing of stress enables the body to function more efficiently, preventing strain from causing general wear and tear.

I also see this herb as a gentle guardian of our Achilles' heel, attending to the weaknesses that become more apparent as we age.

119

This Chinese tonic is becoming more known in the West, especially for the treatment of menopausal symptoms. *Dang gui*, or Chinese angelica, nourishes the blood and encourages circulation. In this way it is very beneficial for menstrual problems such as delayed or painful periods. It relieves the irritability, weepiness, and depression of premenstrual syndrome, helping the menstrual cycle keep a gentle rhythm in the body. Medical research indicates that it helps with an estrogen deficiency, so it may also be a useful herb for menopausal complaints.

CHINESE HERBS

DANG GUI

radix angelicae sinensis

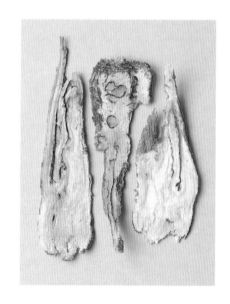

This herb should be avoided during pregnancy. However, after birth it makes an excellent tonic. In China, it is cooked with chicken to create a nourishing, savory dish (see page 129). Combined with another Chinese herb, *huanq qi*, in a decoction, it is a great help with debility and exhaustion. It is also in the Chinese formula, Women's Precious Pills (see page 30).

Dang gui can be used to treat constipation. It is also often used in formulas to treat skin conditions, and is especially helpful for dry skin or ulcers that are not healing.

Free and Easy Wanderer, or Rambling Powder, is a formula derived from the title of the first chapter of *Zhuang Zi* (Rambling without a Destination), which includes stories about soaring above a restricted world view.

This formula releases constraint and encourages the free flowing of the liver *qi*, allowing for open-mindedness, and a free or rambling spirit.

The chief herb of this formula is *chai hui*. Its function is to spread the liver *qi* and release its constraints. The deputies, or negotiators, are *dang gui* and *bai shao*, which work together to nourish the blood and soften the tightness and edginess of the constrained *qi*. The *dang gui* encourages the circulation of blood, which helps to keep the *qi* moving. The assistant herbs, *fu ling*, *bai zhu*, and *zhi gan cao*, strengthen the spleen, which transports and transforms fluids and foods. *Wei jiang*, roasted ginger root, is an envoy, or messenger, that works with the stomach to make the formula more digestible. The other envoy is *bo he*, peppermint, which helps the chief herb to move *qi* and to disperse heat that may come from the stagnation of *qi*.

The focus of this formula is to release constrained *qi*, or encourage a good circulation of energy through the body. In Chinese medicine, the function of the liver is to keep the *qi* moving, and this affects many of our body functions. Stress and tension caused by meeting deadlines, or needing to be in certain places at certain times, can disrupt the natural rhythms in the body, putting the liver under strain. The more demands that are placed on us, the more constraints are put on our liver *qi*, causing us to be irritable and experience headaches, chest pains, vertigo, and fatigue – all symptoms of feeling overwhelmed by life.

Radix bupleuri (chai hu)
Radix angelicae sinensis
  (dang gui)
Radix paeoniae lactiflorae
  (bai shao)
Rhizoma atractylodis
  macrocephalae (bai zhu)
Sclerotium poriae cocos
  (fu ling)
Honey-fried Radix
  glycyrrhizae uralensis (zhi
  gan cao)
Rhizoma zingiberis
  officinalis recens (wei
  jiang)
Herba menthae haplocalycis
  (bo he)

CHANGES FOR MEN

Hormones affect the emotions of men as well as women. The powerful physical and emotional effects of puberty are obvious in young men. As their sexual hormones kick in they can experience mood swings and develop a volatile temper. This often goes unrecognized and invalidated in Western society, which lacks rites of passage for young men and herbal remedies to help them face these challenges.

Good support, schooling, friendships, and diet go a long way to help children in this phase of life. Bach Flower Remedies, which work with the emotions, also have a place. For example, the remedies walnut and wild oats will help guide a young person to find his own direction in life and make the changes needed to get there. Crab apple will help transform negative self-image and encourage a wider outlook. Herbal remedies offer good treatments, which may be an alternative to conventional medicines. Herbs such as valerian, passion flower, and skullcap will offer a relaxing and calming influence during a stressful examination period. Lavender oil in the bath or used in a foot massage will ease anxiety and nervousness. Developing a taste for

herbal teas such as chamomile and peppermint as alternatives to caffeinated teas and coffee will also bring healthy benefits. Cold remedies and those herbs that boost the immune system, such as echinacea, are important as many young people may have periods of feeling run down.

For older men, the male menopause may present itself as a "mid-life crisis" when frustrations at work and in the family might fuel a quest for a new job or relationship. Many men struggle with depression, feelings or sexual inadequacy and impotency during this period of transition. There are herbal remedies that are useful at this time to help to restore balance and revitalize energy, or *qi*. Ginseng is one herb that tonifies *qi* and the yang, supporting more dynamic, masculine energy. Relieving stress and anxiety, its strengthening properties enhance feelings of well-being (see chapter 3 and the Materia Medica, page 170).

A number of herbs that are particularly appropriate to men are featured in this chapter. However, many herbs are beneficial to both men and women, depending on the symptoms, so do look at remedies in other chapters.

This remedy, from the warm climate of the USA, is the fruit or berry of the dwarf palm. In the 1870s, it was observed that animals that ate this plant tended to be heavy and strong. When taken by people, it was discovered that the plant helped to heal reproductive problems, encourage weight gain, and relax the nervous system.

WESTERN HERBS

SAW PALMETTO

serenoa serrulata

BERRIES

Saw palmetto berries have aphrodisiac qualities, helping to increase sexual desire and fertility in both men and women. Symptoms of impotence, amenorrhea, low weight, and fatigue can be relieved with this tonic herb. For men, it is especially helpful in reducing benign prostrate swelling and tenderness. It soothes prostrate and bladder irritations, decreasing incidences of incontinence and dribbling. Toning and strengthening to the male reproductive system, it may be taken safely to boost the male sex hormones.

Damiana leaf is another herb that brings the warmth of the subtropics, where it grows, to strengthen the overall *qi* and *yang* of the body. Strengthening to the male sexual system, it restores the testosterone levels to help prevent impotence and premature ejaculation. Fortifying to the kidney *qi* and soothing to the urinary system, it eases symptoms of incontinence and bladder irritation.

DAMIANA

turnera aphrodisiaca

Damiana is a wonderful nerve tonic and a useful anti-depressant, especially in cases where anxiety and depression are related to sexual problems. It is nourishing to the nervous system, promoting clear thinking, lifting the spirits, and generating strength. It is restoring to conditions of weakness, whether from overwork, illness, or nervous exhaustion. Absent-mindedness and mental dullness are helped by this remarkable herb's ability to stimulate our system.

For women, a combination of damiana leaf and agnus castus taken each morning eases problems such as irregular periods, premenstrual syndrome, and menopausal symptoms accompanied by depression. It is a tonic for the reproductive system, helping with delayed and painful periods. Through its general strengthening effect, it helps to increase sexual interest, and may be considered a mild aphrodisiac.

Damiana may be taken with other herbs, such as saw palmetto berries, for a male tonic. They work together to increase testosterone, encouraging sexual desire and vitality.

The new growth of the chestnut bud heralds the onset of spring. Its remarkable transformation from a brown, sticky bud to soft, downy green leaves is a statement of its power to create change.

CHESTNUT BUD

aesculus hippocastanum

The decision to make a change is based on our desire and our needs. Dr. Bach writes, "our true instincts, desires, likes and dislikes are given us so that we may interpret the spiritual commands of our soul... because the soul alone knows what experiences are necessary for that particular personality." Most of us need to be nudged into these changes, with ill-health and unhappiness acting as turning points in our life.

Chestnut bud is one remedy from a group Dr. Bach made for "Insufficient Interest in Present Circumstances." If we are to understand our patterns and cycles, and to know what is needed to create positive changes in them, we need to be aware of what is going on around us. This remedy helps us to focus on the present situations in our life, so that we do not need to keep repeating old patterns and learning the hard way. It helps us to take full advantage of our experiences, so we can use the wisdom of the past to encourage new beginnings.

WALNUT

juglans regia

HERBS FOR THE SOUL

The walnut tree can grow to a height of 100 ft (30 m), especially in sheltered areas. It gives off a scent that is unattractive to insects and birds, and in this way protects itself. The smell of walnut is particularly strong in the spring when the new buds open into leaf.

This remedy offers protection, especially during times of change. It works well during physical changes such as puberty, pregnancy, and the menopause. It supports us in life decisions or changes in circumstances relating to careers, relationships, births, and deaths of loved ones.

The soft nut within the walnut shell has a resemblance to the brain, and this remedy works with our thought patterns. It releases old ways of thinking, protecting the new beginnings in our life. It brings an immediacy with each new conception that allows them to be nurtured free from the traumas of the past. Protecting us from the enthusiasm, convictions, and strong opinions of others, it leaves us free to follow our own dreams and ambitions.

Walnut is a remedy of freedom for the soul. Dr. Bach writes, "We must gain our freedom absolutely and completely, so that all we do, our every action – nay even our every thought – derives its origin in ourselves, thus enabling us to live and give freely of our own accord, and of our own accord alone."

Scleranthus creeps along the earth, with numerous tangled stems. It grows on sandy or gravelly soils and has clusters of green flowers that burst out from its short leaves. It is an unusual Bach remedy because the flowers have no petals.

FLOWER REMEDIES

SCLERANTHUS

scleranthus annuus

Indecisiveness, fluctuating moods, and poor coordination are all indications that this remedy would be of help. Vacillation, especially between two different choices, gives the symptom picture of a grasshopper making huge, aimless leaps as a response to what happens in the grass. This lack of direction and discrimination comes from not connecting to the deeper aspects of ourself. It is only through the guidance of our inner self that we can direct our actions by the conviction of a deeper purpose.

This remedy brings poise and balance, helping us to move graciously, knowing our true purpose in life. Just as the plant is low-growing in the earth, the remedy reminds us of steadiness and support. With green flowers, the color of the heart chacre, it allows us to open to the insights of the heart. We can then follow our inner rhythm, making decisions with intuitive confidence.

This tall grass has a hairy stem and panicles of seeds that drift in the wind. It is scattered on hedge banks, and the edges of woodlands. The expression "to sow your wild oats" may hold a key that calls us to this remedy, when we need to find our direction in life.

FLOWER REMEDIES

WILD OAT

bromus ramosus

This remedy is indicated when there are many paths before us and we cannot decide which one to take. Instead we may start and stop different projects or relationships, not fully making a commitment to go the distance with them. There is a reluctance to accept that we are on earth for a short period, and to find out what our purpose here is. We may begin to feel restless and dissatisfied with our lives.

Dr. Bach writes, "Let us find the one thing in life that attracts us most and do it. Let that one thing be so part of us that it is as natural as breathing; as natural as it is for the bee to collect honey, and the tree to shed its old leaves in autumn and bring forth new ones in the spring. If we study nature we find that every creature, bird, tree and flower has its definite part to play, its own definite and peculiar work through which it aids and enriches the entire Universe." Wild oat seeks the purpose of our soul and the true meaning of our life's work.

Dang gui, or Chinese angelica, is a blood tonic, which also helps to regulate the hormones. This makes it a useful remedy during the menopause for symptoms such as aches and pains, as well as helping to normalize the cycle. Its warming and moving properties make it a valuable herb to revitalize the circulation, good for cold hands and feet. It helps with symptoms of fatigue, anemia, blurred vision, and minor palpitations. As a carminative herb, it benefits the digestion, and also helps with constipation. Avoid using this herb during pregnancy.

This nourishing recipe revitalizes the *qi* and blood. It is a good tonic after childbirth. Have a bowlful once or twice a week simply to keep you strong and less vulnerable to disease.

3½ pt (2 liters) water
1 medium-sized chicken
¾ oz (20g) *dang gui*
several slices of fresh ginger and root vegetables,
    such as parsnips, carrots, onions, potatoes (optional)

Place all ingredients in a large, non-aluminum pan with a lid. Simmer gently for 1-2 hours until the chicken is completely cooked and there is a good broth. Eat one to two servings a week. Store for up to 24 hours in a refrigerator, or several weeks in a freezer.

Another way of using these ingredients is to prepare Dang Gui Chicken, where the dang gui is baked in the oven alongside the chicken and vegetables. Add extra water or stock to soften the dried dang gui.

DANG GUI CHICKEN SOUP

HERBS
FOR
PROTECTION

Speak to the earth and it shall teach you.

JOB

Through the ages different traditions have used herbs for protection from pestilence and infections, as well as for internal disharmonies of the soul. If we begin to see that there is no separation between the body, mind, and spirit, we can look to the herbs that build up our immune system to help us stay strong in all aspects.

HERBS FOR PROTECTION

According to Chinese medicine, disease comes from external and internal influences. The external influences are wind, cold, heat, damp, and fire. The internal influences are inappropriate joy, anger, fear, worry, and grief. The Chinese believe that the *wei qi*, or defensive energy, runs just beneath the surface of the skin, preventing the wind from penetrating the body and bringing with it external influences that destabilize the harmonious flow of energy. It is the *wei qi*, then, that protects the *qi*, or life-force. There is no equivalent defensive energy against the internal influences. Instead, moderation and control of joy, anger, fear, worry, and grief are the best protection against disease.

In Western medicine research has shown the importance of the immune system, which fights off infections.

These are often caused by viruses and bacteria that pass through the air we breathe. When we are tired, or low in energy, we are more susceptible to catching a cold or flu. Sometimes our immunity breaks down and we experience a series of infections, unable to completely recover and regain our strength. Herbs are an effective treatment for building up the immune system.

There are, of course, situations when it is advisable to use antibiotics, and they save many lives. However, we need to recognize their shortcomings and use them with discretion. Herbal treatment can be taken alongside antibiotics. You may need to take some herbs to clear symptoms that are left over from an illness, such as catarrh (see chapter five). Fatigue may be the result of an illness; if this is the case, take some tonic herbs to renew your vitality (see chapter three). Some herbs have several benefits, for example, echinacea clears catarrh and builds up the immune system, offering protection from repeated infections. The herbs in this chapter are useful for building up immunity in all circumstances.

In addition to taking herbs, our ancestors employed other methods of protecting themselves from the ravages of ill health. During the Middle Ages, for instance, thyme and rosemary were burned because their smoke was believed to repel the pestilence of the plague. The druids scattered herbs such as meadowsweet and chamomile around the room so that their gentle scents would promote a peaceful atmosphere. The practice of burning herbs or incense to cleanse and purify the air is an essential part of many rituals and traditions.

"Smudging" is the traditional way for Native Americans to purify themselves and cleanse the air. Burning certain herbs, such as sage, cedar, and sweetgrass clears negativity to create a lighter, more positive space. Small, green cedar branches are especially effective for clearing negativity and bad thoughts. Sweetgrass is a gentle, scented herb, often burned after the sage and cedar to call for the blessing of good spirits. Performing these rituals with the herbs is a way of honoring the soul and offering it protection.

The herbs need to be dried, so that they will burn easily. They can be bought or gathered and dried. When gathering the herbs, it is important to make sure that you only take a small part of the plant and give thanks for its gift. Place the dried herbs in a small fireproof bowl and light them. They should light easily. Thank the herbs for their healing and ask for their help with the cleansing and clearing that needs to be done. Wave the smoke over yourself, starting with your face and going down to your feet. The smoke can be directed with your hands or with a feather. With the help of another person, wave the sage smoke over your head and down your back. When you have finished, let the herbs burn safely down. When they are cold, return the ashes the earth with a prayer of thanks.

Visualization can help cleanse and strengthen our aura, the field of energy that surrounds the body. Close your eyes and relax by taking several deep breaths. Visualize a pure white light shining around you. Feel the warmth of the light, and see its rays penetrating your aura, revitalizing places where you feel weak and vulnerable. Concentrate on this for five to ten minutes, breathing slowly. Then give thanks to the universe for this healing light.

This simple plant is related to southernwood and wormwood. All are different types of *Artemisia*, named after the Greek moon goddess Artemis. Artemis revived the plants at night with her refreshing dew, while her twin brother Apollo encouraged their growth with the sun's rays. A goddess for women, Artemis held their protection in her hands, and offered healing for their fertility, menstrual cycle, and childbirth.

MUGWORT

artemisia vulgaris

Mugwort is said to protect travellers from harm. In the Middle Ages the plant was known as *Cingulum Sancti Johannis*, and was believed to have been worn in the girdle of John the Baptist when he journeyed through the wilderness. It protected wanderers from fatigue, sunstroke, wild beasts, and evil spirits.

Medicinally, mugwort has a long tradition of healing menstrual problems, increasing fertility, and aiding childbirth. It is a good digestive stimulant because its bitterness increases the gastric juices. It has a mild action on the nervous system, relieving tensions and depression. Used for centuries for epilepsy, nervousness, and fright, it was valued for fits and convulsions, especially in people of weak constitution.

The leaves of this herb are used in the Chinese medicinal treatment called moxibustion. They are rolled into sticks, like cigars, or used in small cones that are placed directly on the skin. The mugwort, or moxa, is lit and a warming heat penetrates deep into the body. It is used to strengthen and warm the energy, encouraging a good circulation to certain areas, or specific acupuncture points. It is very healing for complaints such as cold aching joints, stiff muscles, and cramping pains. I use it on a point below the knee to tonify the immune system and offer protection and strength. It is especially effective for children.

GARLIC

This powerful remedy has been used in many traditions of herbal medicine. An ancient Egyptian papyrus dating from 1500 B.C. records its use for headaches, throat infections, and weakness. It was given to the builders of the pyramids to strengthen and energize them. The ancient Greeks also believed that garlic was a symbol of strength and it was chewed by athletes at the Olympic games to improve their performances. Its name comes from the Anglo-Saxon word *gar* meaning spear and *lac* meaning plant. The name refers to its qualities and the straight green shoots that form its leaves.

Garlic has a reputation for warding off infections and evil influence. Its strong link to magic and the occult can be seen in China, where there is a tradition of hanging garlic from the roofs of houses to protect against evil. Translations from early medicinal texts relate the causes of disease to "evil influences" such as cold, heat, and wind, as well as anger, joy, and sorrow. Diseases of both the mind and the body are still seen in these terms in a modern Chinese diagnosis.

The medicinal properties of this plant are wide-ranging and very effective. It is strengthening and revitalizing, helping to build a good immune system. It fights against bacterial and viral infections and dispels parasites. The strongly scented volatile oil is largely excreted via the lungs, clearing chest infections and recurring colds. Raw garlic, when crushed, releases allicin, which has been shown to be a more powerful antibiotic than penicillin.

Garlic has a long traditional use as a remedy for heart disease and high blood pressure. Recent research indicates garlic's effectiveness at lowering harmful levels of cholesterol, making it a good treatment for arteriosclerosis and high blood pressure. It reduces blood pressure and a tendency for clotting, which is helpful in the prevention of strokes.

It encourages good circulation and, being warming in its nature, is good for poor circulation and cold hands and feet.

Although most modern herbals have no cautions or contraindications for garlic, I have found Culpepper's warning to have some truth, "Many authors quote many diseases garlic is good for, but conceal its vices." Garlic has very hot properties so should be used with care by those whose nature and body temperature is warm or hot, and taken in small doses.

The name of this woody, green herb with its sweet, cleansing scent is derived from the Latin *salvus*, meaning well-being. It has a strong connection to wisdom and longevity, and during the Middle Ages was an ingredient in the concoctions that were considered the elixirs of life. Considered a tonic to strengthen the brains and the nerves, it restored the mind, memory, and virility. It was prescribed for depression, insomnia, and nervous exhaustion, as well as a convalescence remedy for the elderly. Culpepper writes, "Sage is of excellent use to help the memory, warming and quickening the senses."

WESTERN HERBS

SAGE

salvia officinalis

Sage is a deep-acting herb that enhances our immunity and restores balance to our nervous system and mental functions. It helps with long-term fatigue, excessive sweating, dizziness, forgetfulness, and depression. A useful remedy for the menopause, sage can be a great support with exhaustion, nightsweats, hot flushes, and signs of mental fatigue. Avoid drinking sage tea if pregnant or breast-feeding.

As an antiseptic and anti-bacterial remedy, it fights skin infections and is also good for sore throats, inflamed gums, and mouth ulcers. Sage soothes and heals insect bites and stings. Prepare an infusion of sage tea, and use it as a wash on affected areas, or as a gargle.

White mountain sage is a traditional herb used by Native Americans to cleanse and clear negativity from a room or person. It is burned as a smudge; its smoke and scent clearing difficult emotions and energies and bringing a sense of lightness and peace.

Tea tree is a small tree, with narrow leaves and yellow flowers. The bark of the tree, known as paperbark, is easy to peel off and is used by the aboriginal peoples of Australia to make canoes and as thatching for houses. The pungent leaves are soaked in hot water and taken as a cure for colds, coughs, and headaches, or are simply picked and chewed.

WESTERN HERBS

TEA TREE

melaleuca alternifolia

Tea tree, with its valuable cleansing and healing properties, is added to shampoo, skin conditioners, and toothpaste. It clears toxicity, reduces infections, and stimulates immunity. Like marigold, it has anti-bacterial, antiviral, and antifungal properties, though tea tree is the stronger at fighting infections.

Tea tree has a very pungent odor, and the volatile oil helps to clear phlegm and relieve coughing. It is excellent in a steam inhalation, especially if there are signs of a chest infection. Use it to clear sinusitis, bronchitis, laryngitis, and flu. Like the Chinese herb, *huang qi*, it strengthens the defensive *qi*, building up the immune system and protecting against recurring infections. Use tea tree oil sparingly – a little goes a long way.

Tea tree restores the nerves and encourages blood flow to the brain, promoting clear thinking and relieving depression. Its sharp odor cuts through confusion, overcoming fatigue and absent-mindedness. Fortifying to the soul, it focuses positive thinking and the healing instinct. A remedy of special value to physically delicate individuals who tend to feel victimized and doomed by chronic ill-health, it offers protection in many ways, and supports a clear and positive outlook.

This magnificent tree is native to Japan and China. It has one or more trunks and fan-shaped leaves. In China, where it endured the last ice age, it was planted at powerful sites connected with the worship of ancestors, around tombs, and near temples. It was one of the few plants to survive the bombing of Hiroshima during World War II.

WESTERN HERBS

gingko biloba

GINGKO

Recent research confirms many of its uses in Chinese medicine. It has become increasingly popular as a remedy to improve age-related dementia, promoting good memory and clear thinking. It encourages good circulation, especially to the brain, helping with absent-mindedness, dizziness, and tinnitus.

Gingko revitalizes the blood flow so it can be used for varicose veins, cramping, and aching legs. The heart also benefits from its restorative effect on circulation. It eases chest pain and shortness of breath.

The gingko tree has survived traumatic events over the centuries and knows how to protect itself. Modern research also indicates that it offers us protection from premature aging. This herb decreases the damage caused by environmental toxins, especially chemical pollution. Taken preventatively, it will encourage good health into old age. Treatment needs to last for several months to see noticeable improvement. It you are taking medication for circulatory conditions, consult a herbalist before using gingko.

This formula strengthens the *wei qi*, a protective energy that runs just beneath the skin. It serves as a barrier against the wind which, according to Chinese medicine, can bring in the cold or heat and affect our energy. This formula is considered to be as valuable and precious as the jade after which it is named.

YU PING

jade screen powder

FENG SAN

*Radix astragali
    membranacei (huang qi)*
*Rhizoma atractylodis
    macrocephalae (bai zhu)*
*Radix ledebouriellae
    divaricatae (fang feng)*

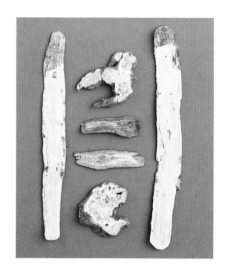

The chief herb is *huang qi*, which is powerful in its function to protect and stabilize the *wei qi*. *Bai zhu* supports it by strengthening the spleen, which supports our internal *qi*, or energy, and is also a tonic for the lungs. Together they work to prevent pathogens from entering the body. The *fang feng* is the assistant herb; it circulates the exterior of the body expelling wind and pathogens. It does this by working with the *huang qi* and *bai zhu*, so it does not harm the body's energy.

There are several symptoms that indicate this formula is an appropriate one to take. It can be used, for instance, to prevent recurring colds, coughs, or sore throats, making us less susceptible to infections. Through its effect on the skin pores, it can also be used to prevent excessive sweating. I use it with clients who have been susceptible to drafts, suffering a recurring neck or shoulder ache from cold breezes. It is an effective remedy for many allergic conditions, such as hay fever and rhinitis, but is best taken before the season when the allergies are at their worst.

This beneficial Chinese herb is strengthening to the immune system. It works with the *wei qi*, or defensive *qi*, which flows just beneath the skin, working to protect the body from outside influences such as cold, wind, and dampness. It is part of the remedy used in the treatment of AIDS and cancer to build up some immunity to infections. *Huang qi* raises the *qi* and in this way works to lift our spirits, making this a useful remedy for depression, especially if it is due to weakness.

This remedy builds up the digestive function, encouraging a good appetite, effective bowel function, and relieving tiredness. It strengthens the lungs, and also works with the pores of the skin, closing them to prevent excessive perspiration, or opening them to encourage sweating to clear colds and flus. As mentioned above, it has a lifting energy, and can be the appropriate remedy for prolapses of the uterus or rectum. It is a widely used remedy in many Chinese formulas as it is strengthening to the mind and spirit, as well as many parts of the body.

HOLLY

ilex aquifolium

A strong evergreen tree, well-known for its spiny leaves, the holly creates an impenetrable forest. In the center of a holly grove you can feel the protective strength of the trees. In the traditions of the Romans, druids, and Christian church, this tree offers protection from evil, or the negative influences that can possess us. Associated with Candlemas, or Christmas, it offers light and hope in the darkness of winter. Much like the Christos, it carries the transformative power of divine love.

Where the walnut tree protects us from outside influences, this tree helps us when we are overcome with negativity, envy, hatred, jealousy, and rage. If we are conscious of these emotions, we can counteract them by opening our hearts to the love that is there for us. Living in a state of grace, our heart is open and we are one with all things. If we cannot accept this love, we move into the opposite feelings of negativity, separation, and hatred.

Holly acts to reunite us with our soul, to drive out these negative emotions, and fill us with love. Dr. Bach writes, "The ultimate conquest of all will be through love and gentleness, and when we have sufficiently developed these two qualities nothing will be able to assail us, since we shall ever have compassion and not offer resistance....Holly protects us from everything that is not Universal Love. Holly opens the heart and unites us with Divine Love."

144

This delicious recipe for garlic syrup is sweet and soothing. It was once a popular remedy for asthma. It can still be used for this and also taken for coughs, hoarseness, and other chest complaints. Garlic fights against infections and helps to clear the phlegm.

RECIPE

GARLIC SYRUP

1 cup (250ml) boiling water
4oz (125g) garlic, peeled and sliced
1 tablespoon fennel seed, crushed
$\frac{1}{4}$ cup (70ml) vinegar
8oz (250g) sugar

Add the boiling water to the garlic, cover and let stand for 12–24 hours. In a small pan, simmer the fennel seed in the vinegar. Add this to the garlic mixture and stir well. Heat this mixture and simmer until the garlic is soft. Strain through a piece of muslin, pressing the garlic to extract all the juices. Heat the liquid and gradually add the sugar. Stir constantly to dissolve the sugar, taking care not to allow the mixture to boil. Allow the syrup to cool then pour into sterilized bottles. Store in a cool, dark place. Take up to three teaspoons a day when needed.

LOVE

POTIONS

Wherever you are,
Whatever your condition is,
Always try to be a lover.

RUMI

The five-petaled wild rose is associated with
Christ on earth because it forms the human shape
with arms spread out and legs apart, which fits
into a five-petaled star. It therefore represents
divine love in its earthly form.

RONI JAY

LOVE POTIONS

Love potions and spells have been part of many traditions for centuries, and a good number of these involve the use of flowers or herbs. Flowers hold the language of love, and can express affection when words fail. The beauty of their colors and the sweetness of their scent carry their message to the soul. Some flowers, such as orchids, roses, jasmine, and orange blossom, carry the messages of love and fertility, and were often woven into bridal bouquets and garlands. Basil, marjoram, and rosemary are associated with love and fidelity and are used to strengthen the ceremony of marriage. Climbing vines of jasmine, honeysuckle, and ivy are also symbolic of marriage and partnership as they entwine round each other like lover's arms.

Roses have a long association with love. In Greek mythology, this special flower was created from the body of a nymph. The Three Graces gave it joy, brilliance, and charm; Aphrodite, the goddess of love, blessed the flower with beauty; and Dionysus, the god of wine, added nectar to give it a special fragrance. The rose, the queen of flowers, was born and became the symbol of love.

The compassion of this flower lies in its ability to heal old emotional wounds, especially those that have grown out of hurt and rejection. This remedy offers love and nurturing for oneself, which is the beginning point to finding true love. Its sweet, gentle comfort brings healing to the deepest despair and restores the trust that makes it possible to love again.

Here are some love potions dedicated to the rose. A single red rose carries a suitor's passion and affection. Bathe in rose buds to conjure a lover. Place roses in a red cloth bag and pin it under your clothes to attract the love of your life, or make a necklace out of rose hips instead of beads.

Lavender is calming and stabilizing to the heart. As John Gerard wrote in 1597, lavender "doth help the passion and panting of the heart." While this may be part of our sense of excitement in love, we may at times need to find a way of not being overwhelmed by a new relationship. In 1660, Richard Surflet wrote that the "distilled water of the flowers restoreth the lost speech, and healeth the swoonings and disease of the heart." So if we need to be a bit more rational and calm about our love, this is the herb to use.

LAVENDER

lavendula officinalis

Within the Celtic tradition, lavender was burned in bonfires as an offering to the Gods and Goddesses at midsummer. It was used in love spells, as its scent was said to attract men.

For a spell, choose a herb with care and give thanks to the Earth for her gift. Place it in a chalice, a ritual cup, or in your pocket. Call to the harmonizing and restoring spirit of lavender, with a prayer, asking for help with your relationship. Send your thanks, then cast the lavender into the air, water, or fire, or bury it in earth.

ROSEMARY

rosemarinus officinalis

"Seethe much rosemary," advised William Langham (1597) "and bathe therein to make thee lusty, lively, joyfull, likeing and youngly." This strong-scented herb is invigorating and stimulating, encouraging vitality and spark. Physically, it strengthens the heartbeat and encourages a good circulation. It is an exhilarating herb, ruled by the sun, a symbol of warmth, strength, and light.

Shakespeare refers to this herb when Hamlet tells Ophelia, "Here's rosemary for remembrance...I pray you love remember." The traditional use for rosemary was to strengthen the memory, and it has become known as a herb of loyalty and fidelity. In southern European countries, a sprig of rosemary is placed in the slippers of the bride and groom so that they will remain loyal to one another. Woven into the bride's bouquet it brings joy and luck.

viscum album

MISTLETOE

Mistletoe's iridescent white berries ripen in mid-winter, ignoring the rhythms and laws of the seasons. The ripe berries, green berries, open flowers and immature leaves all appear together, not adhering to the growing sequence of most plants. It will grow upside down, sideways, or in any direction, and germinates in the light rather than the dark. Defying conventions, it is said to belong to the interval between dusk and dawn. Mistletoe is poisonous if taken internally and has therefore been omitted from the Materia Medica.

The Scandinavian legend of Baldur is just one of many tales about this magical herb. Baldur, the "shining" god was troubled by dreams of his death. Frigg, the mother of the gods, asked all living beings to take a pledge to not kill him, but she forgot to ask the mistletoe. One of the old gods, a playful troublemaker called Loki, put a sprig of mistletoe into the hands of Hodur, who was blind. The gods were making a game of throwing things at Baldur, knowing that he would not be hurt and was protected from harm. Hodur hurled the branch of mistletoe at Baldur, and killed him. The earth was plunged into mourning at the death of Baldur, who held such beauty in his shining spirit, sinking into spiritual darkness – a "dark winter of the soul." Because Baldur was loved by all the other gods and goddesses, they pleaded for him to be restored to life. When he was, mistletoe was placed under the protection of the goddess of love, and it was ordained that all who passed under it should kiss, to show that the mistletoe had become an emblem of love. This is why we can embrace our tradition of kissing under the mistletoe at Christmas, to honor its holding by the goddess of love, and the return of light after the longest night of the winter solstice.

BASIL
ocimum basilicum

Basil is a sacred plant of India and has been used for healing for thousands of years. Basil opens the heart and the mind, bestowing love and devotion. Sacred to Vishnu and Krishna, it strengthens faith, compassion, and clarity. In the Celtic tradition, basil was used to mend lovers' quarrels and in love spells. If the dried herb is sprinkled over the heart it is said to promote fidelity. Basil is also believed to create understanding between people. Drink it as a tea, use the oil in a burner, or keep a plant in the house.

MYRTLE
myrtus communis

Myrtle, a flower of love, is sacred to the goddess Aphrodite, or Venus. After Aphrodite's birth, she stepped from the waves to the land and hid in the cover of myrtle bushes. From then on she wore a wreath of myrtle on her head, and bushes were planted around her temples. Grow a myrtle bush outside your door to bring love and beauty to your home.

Marjoram's nourishing qualities offer strength and support when we are feeling depleted or under stress. For those times when we feel isolated or alone, whether this is real or imagined, it brings warmth and comfort. Calming obsessive thinking and easing emotional craving, it allows us to find our inner capacity for self-nurturing. As a herb of love, marjoram nourishes our neediness, helping restore compassion for ourself and others.

MARJORAM

origanum vulgare

WESTERN HERBS

Marjoram, according to Greek mythology, is the creation of Aphrodite, whose gentle touch gave the herb its scent. In Roman myths, it is the flower sacred to Venus. It was woven into crowns and worn in both cultures by newlyweds, symbolic of fertility, love, and honor.

Mrs Grieve offers this love potion from Halliwell's *Popular Rhymes and Superstitions:*

> "On St. Luke's Day, says Mother Bunch, take marigold flowers, a sprig of marjoram, thyme and a little wormwood; dry them before a fire, rub them to powder, then sift it through a fine piece of lawn, and simmer it over a slow fire, adding a small quantity of virgin honey and vinegar. Anoint yourself with this when you go to bed, saying the following lines three times, and you will dream of your future partner 'that is to be.'
> St. Luke, St. Luke, be kind to me,
> In dreams let me my true love see.
> If a girl desires to obtain this information, let her seek for a green peascod in which there are nine peas, and write on a piece of paper-
> Come in, my dear,
> And do not fear:
> which paper she must enclose in the peascod, and lay it under the door. The first person who comes into the room will be her husband."

WESTERN HERBS

MEADOWSWEET

filipendula ulmaria

Meadowsweet, watermint, and vervain were three herbs held most sacred by the druids. Another name for meadowsweet is "queen of the meadow" or "bride of the meadow." Its tall clumps of gentle white blossom catch the sun and release a fragrance of honey and almonds. It has associations with the Celtic goddess Brighid. She carried the flame through the winter darkness into the early spring light, inspiring poets and craftsmen with her beauty. Venus governs this herb, and it is used in love potions, as well as to "make the heart merrie."

Yarrow has a long association with magic. Its name is derived from the Greek *hieros* which means sacred. Found preserved in temples, it was thought to be endowed with spiritual properties, and was used as a charm against negative energies. As a herb that awakened visions, yarrow stalks were thrown in the ancient Chinese oracle, the *I Ching*.

Yarrow is said to be ruled by Venus, the planet of love. In traditional folklore, a girl who places a stalk of yarrow under her pillow and repeats this verse will dream of her future husband:

Thou pretty herb of Venus Tree
Thy true name is Yarrow
Now who my bosom friend must be
Pray tell me thou tomorrow.
HALLIWELL'S POPULAR RHYMES
AND SUPERSTITIONS

WU WEI ZI

fructus schisandrae chinensis

This Chinese herb is a famous sex tonic for both women and men.
It reinforces the energy, or *jing qi*, of the kidneys, which supports vitality
and reproduction. Chinese women have used this herb for centuries
because it encourages the production of body fluids that soften and
beautify the skin. Modern research shows that it has an exciting and
sedating effect that helps to balance the nervous system and bring a
good night's sleep. As a tonic, it increases endurance and reduces
fatigue.

Here is an easy recipe to make a scented soap with lavender flowers. These tiny lilac-colored flowers have a powerful aromatic fragrance which relaxes us into a state of well-being. Tensions and anxieties disappear so we are able to "be in the moment" and feel the joy of our love for another. The beauty of lavender is in its harmonizing properties, its fragrance being appreciated by both men and women. It has a balancing influence on both sexes, enhancing a certain gentleness in men, while bringing a tendancy towards greater strength in women.

RECIPE

LAVENDER SOAP

2 tablespoons of fresh lavender flowers, chopped
2 tablespoons of glycerine, warmed
12 tablespoons of olive-oil-based soap, grated
1 tablespoon of clear honey
ribbon (optional)
several extra sprigs of lavender flowers (optional)

Place the chopped lavender flowers in the warmed glycerine and leave to infuse in a warm place for 2 hours. This softens the flowers and lets the fragrance and healing properties of lavender mix into the glycerine. Melt the soap in a heatproof bowl placed over a saucepan of boiling water. Remove from the heat and add the mixture of glycerine and lavender flowers. Add the honey. Pour the soaps into molds greased with glycerine and leave to set. Remove from molds when set. For decoration, wrap a ribbon around the soap and tie on a sprig of lavender.

HERBAL

PREPARATIONS

There is only one active ingredient in plant medicines – friendship. A plant spirit heals a patient as a favour to its friend in dreaming, the doctor.

ELIOT COWAN

HERBAL PREPARATIONS

There are many ways to take herbs and receive their benefits. Herbal teas, or infusions, have a refreshing taste and are a healing remedy. They are easy to prepare from herbs in the garden or tea bags from stores. Certain herbs – usually roots, barks, or seeds – will need to be simmered gently to obtain their goodness, and this is known as a decoction. Chinese herbal prescriptions are prepared in this way, as they need this gentle cooking to break down the herbs into their medicinal components. Some people may prefer to take herbs in pills or in tinctures, where they are concentrated in an alcohol base. Traditional preparations also include herbal wines, syrups, vinegars, and using herbs in cooking.

Herbal baths are a relaxing and rejuvenating way of enjoying the benefits of the plants. Use simple hand and foot baths to experience their healing nature. Prepare oils infused with herbs for massage. Gentle stroking or a more vigorous massage can be enhanced by using these oils directly on the skin. Make herbal inhalations for an effective treatment for complaints of cold, cough and flu. They also help to restore a deep, calm breath.

gathering herbs

Gathering herbs can be a quest that brings healing in itself. Native American teachings speak of searching for healing herbs in a sacred way. Realizing that each herb is a gift from Grandmother Earth, a prayer of thanks is given before picking the herb. With this, they state that the herb is to be used for healing and ask its permission to use it in this way. They make sure that there is still plenty of the plant left, so the herb can regrow. In Plant Spirit Medicine, which comes from this traditional shamanism, the spirit of the plant is recognized and asked for help in healing.

Many herbs are found in fields, woods, and gardens. Being able to identify the correct herb is important so follow a description in a field guide or go out with someone who knows plants. Some herbs are usually known as weeds. Nettles, couch grass, and dandelion all contain excellent medicinal properties, although they are not welcome in most gardens. There are other species such as lavender, marigold, and lemon balm that are more commonly grown in a herbal garden.

There are a few guidelines to follow when herbs are gathered. They ensure that herbs will always be there for everyone's use and that you make best use of them.

- Check carefully in a field guide to make sure that the plant you are choosing is the herb you need.
- Do not uproot plants or deplete the area of a herb. It is better to take a small selection home and let the rest multiply.
- Make sure that the plant is not a rare or protected species.
- Choose healthy herbs that have not been exposed to pesticides or insect damage.
- Do not gather herbs near busy roads or industrial sites.
- Know which part of the herb you need. With some plants, the roots, leaves, and flowers have different uses.
- Gather the herb after the dew has dried, but before the sun is at full strength, to ensure its constituents are most potent.
- Know the growing cycle of the herb, so that it is gathered at the time when its medicinal value is of greatest potency. It is sensible to consult a field guide to discover the optimum time for gathering them.

Generally roots of perennial herbs are harvested in the autumn when the foliage has died down and the goodness has returned to the roots. It is best to wait until their second or more year of flowering. Marshmallow roots are dug in mid-autumn while valerian roots are harvested in late autumn.

The leaves of the plants are best harvested in the spring. Collect them midmorning, after the dew has dried but before the sun draws out their essential oils. Most herbs contain the greatest amount of essential oils just before they flower. Only leaves of perfect quality should be harvested, leaving those with insect damage or disease. With thyme and rosemary, gather the leaves just as the first flowers are about to open, as this makes a difference to the taste. Do not wait until the flowers have begun to die off. Marshmallow is an exception; the leaves should be gathered when the flowers are open.

Flowers are harvested at their height of bloom. Choose those that are in good condition. Buds are collected as they are beginning to swell. They will open more as they dry.

Seeds are collected when the seed pod is formed,

just before they reach maturity. They are left to ripen fully as they are dried. Hang them upside down with a paper bag or soft cloth wrapped around them. The seeds fall into the bag or cloth as they dry.

drying and storing herbs

Fresh herbs need to be used quickly to take full advantage of their goodness. After several days they start to decay unless they are dried properly. Drying and storing herbs is easy, but requires a

space that is warm, dry, and out of direct sunlight. To dry herbs, spread them on a piece of brown paper or on a rack and place them in a warm, dry cupboard. Spread them so that the leaves and flower heads do not overlap and the air can circulate around them. Leave them to dry for one to three weeks. If mold appears, it means there is too much moisture and not enough air moving around them. The herbs should be thrown away. Start again with a new batch of herbs, repeating the process. When drying is completed the leaves should be like paper, fragile, but not so dry that they powder when touched. Avoid drying strong smelling herbs next to others as their flavor spreads through their fragrance.

Alternatively, herbs can be hung in an attic or a dark corner of the kitchen. Sage, rosemary, and thyme can be dried by hanging small bunches of leaves by their stems. Tie about 5–10 stems together. Do not pack them too tightly, as air needs to circulate around each bunch.

When collecting small flowers such as lavender, hang bunches of four or five stems in a dry place, with the flower heads in a small paper bag. Make sure the bag covers the flowers entirely so they are caught in the bag as they fall off the stems. Seedheads, such as fennel and dill, can also be collected this way. Otherwise dry them over a tray that will catch the seeds as they fall.

Roots can be cleaned and cut into small pieces, about 1–2 centimeters thick. Pat these on an absorbent towel, then place them in the oven on a baking tray. Bake at a low heat, about 120°F (50°C), until they become brittle, keeping the oven door ajar. Check at intervals to see if they are soft, which means that they still contain moisture. Allow them to dry slowly at a low temperature. Higher temperatures may destroy some of their delicate constituents. They will take several hours to dry thoroughly.

Herbs should be stored in airtight bottles away from sunlight, moisture, and dust. Plastic and metal containers are not suitable as they may affect the chemistry of the herbs. To store leaves, pick them off the stem when dried. Try to place them in a container as a whole leaf – this will help them retain their scent and goodness longer. Crush them before using. Seeds, flowers, and roots can also be stored in dark, airtight containers. Label bottles with the name of the herb and the date it was stored. Check them at intervals for moisture, molds, and insects. Throw them away if there is any damage. Most leaves and flowers lose their medicinal potency after a year, at which time there is a new season to harvest. Seeds and roots can be stored for two to three years.

infusions

Infusions or teas are a well-known way of taking herbal medicine. They are used with the more delicate parts of plants – leaves, seeds, and flowers – which release their medicinal qualities into the water. Dry or fresh herbs can be used. Fresh herbs have a higher medicinal value, but dry herbs are often more readily available and can be obtained all year long. Because of the moisture in fresh herbs, you will need to use more.

To make a hot infusion in a pot, choose a pot that has not been used for black tea because the tannin residue will overpower the ingredients of herbal teas. Prepare the pot by first warming it, then place the herbs in it and add freshly boiled water. Use 1 $\frac{1}{4}$ pt (600 ml) of boiling water and approximately 1 oz (20 g) of dried, or 1 $\frac{1}{2}$ oz (30 g) of fresh herbs. Leave the herbs to steep for 10–15 minutes. Make sure that the pot is covered to retain the vitamins and volatile oils. The tea may be drunk hot or cold, and with honey, if preferred. One pot of tea will make approximately three cups. It may be kept for up to 24 hours.

An infusion made in a cup is prepared in a similar way. Use approximately 1–2 tsp (2 g) of dried, or 2–3 tsp (3 g) of fresh herbs per cup. Place the herbs in a tea strainer on the cup and pour over freshly boiled water until it covers the herbs. Cover the cup and leave the tea for 10–15 minutes. Add honey if preferred.

decoctions

A decoction is used to prepare a herbal tea that contains barks, roots, or berries. The contents of the herbs are more difficult to extract and need to be simmered in water. The sections of root or bark should be chopped as finely as possible. Place 1 oz (20 g) of dried, or 2 oz (40 g) of fresh herb in about 1 $\frac{1}{2}$ pints (750 ml) of cold water in a non-aluminum pan with a lid. Ideally they should soak for 15 minutes to soften the herbs to release their goodness, but this is not always necessary. Bring to a boil quickly, then simmer gently for 10 minutes on very low heat. Allow the preparation to cool to drinking temperature, then strain, pressing out as much liquid from the herbs as possible.

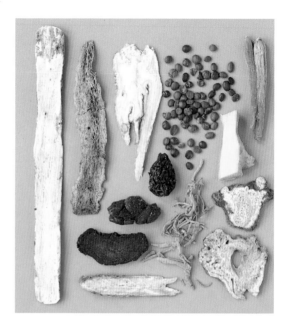

If you wish to combine two herbs, for example, a root and flower or leaf, add the flower or leaf at the end of the simmering. Then let the decoction sit for 10 minutes, covered, to absorb the medicinal properties.

Decoctions are generally made in larger quantities and can be kept for longer because the tea is sterilized in the boiling process. They will keep refrigerated for up to three days. A small amount can be warmed up or set out to stand at room temperature before drinking. Add honey, if preferred.

chinese herbal decoctions

Chinese herbs are always prepared as decoctions because roots, berries, and seeds are more commonly used in these medicinal brews. Chinese herbalists will recommend different ways of preparing the herbs depending on their own methods and the herbs used. Use a non-aluminum pot with a lid. Cover the dried herbs with water. Generally the herbs will need to soak for up to one hour, then be simmered for 30–45 minutes. For specific instructions on the dosage and preparation of individual herbs, see the Materia Medica (page 170).

chinese herbal pills

Many of the traditional Chinese herbal formulas come in pill form. These are easy to take. However, their effect is not so strong, and it is not possible to tailor them to an individual's exact needs as you can with dried herbs. Consult a Chinese herbalist for the most suitable formula. Dosages depend on the brand name and are usually included on the label. Start with the smallest dose listed and take for one week. If there are no problems, increase the dose and take over a longer period of time to feel their benefits.

tinctures

A tincture is a herbal preparation that is based in alcohol and water. Some herbs lend themselves readily to tinctures because the alcohol is warming and easily absorbed into the system. Mostly tinctures are used because they are easy to take, do not involve much preparation (many are readily available in health stores), and do not taste too strong. For many children it is the easiest way to take a herbal preparation. Tinctures last for up to two years, so they are a very convenient way to take herbal medicine over a long period of time.

Herbal tinctures are stronger than infusions and decoctions, and they are taken in teaspoons or milliliters depending on the herb used or the amount needed. By using a dropper bottle, the amount can be measured by 20 drops equalling 1ml. Generally doses are between 1–5 ml three times a day. It is important to check the individual dosage of each herb in the Materia Medica (page 170), and take it according to the age requirements.

To make a herbal tincture, take 8 oz (227 g) of dried herbs and chop them finely. Put them in a glass vessel or jar with a tight-fitting lid. Add $\frac{1}{2}$ pt (250 ml) of vodka, gin, or brandy. The alcohol should be at least 30 percent proof in order to preserve the herbs. Then add $1\frac{1}{2}$ pt (750 ml) of water. So the liquid is made up of 25 percent alcohol and 75 percent water. Place the covered jar in a warm, dark place for 14 days. Shake the mixture every two or three days. Strain the mixture through double muslin, squeezing out as much of the liquid as possible from the herbs. Store in a well-stoppered dark glass jar in a cupboard.

dosages

Herbs are potent forms of medicine. They must be taken carefully and in the right dosage. The dosage will depend on the method of preparation, the herb used, and the age of the person taking the herb. When following dosages and recipes, it is important to stay with one system of measurement, either metric or imperial. Herbs can be very useful during pregnancy, but it is important to check in the Materia Medica (see page 170) to see if a herb is safe to use during this period. Specific dosages for each herb are also included in the Materia Medica. They should be followed carefully. Cautions and contraindications are also listed there. Please check them carefully before taking any herbs, especially if you are pregnant or on medication.

Babies – Remedies should be prescribed by a herbal practitioner. Breast-feeding mothers can take the normal dose and the infant will receive the appropriate amount, but herbs should be checked by a herbal practitioner to make sure they are beneficial to both the mother and child.

Children of one to six years old - Remedies can be taken as one-third the normal adult dosage.

Children of six to 12 years – Remedies can be taken as one-half the normal adult dosage.

Adults – Infusions, or herbal teas, can be drunk as two to four cups (8 fl oz/227 mls) a day. Decoctions can be taken as two to three cupfuls a day. Tinctures are measured in milliliters (ml). Use a dropper bottle – 20 drops = 1 ml. Take the recommended dosage two to three times a day in small amounts of water or juice.

Over 70s – Cupfuls of infusions, or herbal teas can be drunk two to three times a day. Decoctions can be taken as one to two cupfuls daily. Take the recommended dosage of tinctures twice a day in a small amount of water or juice.

Medicinal wines are usually taken by the sherry glassful (approximately $2\frac{1}{2}$ fl oz/70 ml). One glassful is taken daily. Syrups , on the other hand, are taken by the teaspoonful. One to three teaspoonfuls may be taken up to three times a day.

medicinal wines

Medicinal wines have a long tradition of use in both Chinese and Western herbal medicine. The alcohol is warming and invigorating to the circulation. It helps the herbs to be assimilated easily into the body. It is also a good way of preserving herbs. Herbs can be added to bottled wine, preferably organic, or a more traditional approach is to brew the wine with the herbs.

To add herbs to bottled wine, use 4 oz (100 g) of dried herbs to a $\frac{1}{2}$ pt (1 liter) of wine. Place the herbs in a glass jar that has a tight-fitting lid and pour the wine on top. Seal the jar and leave for up to two weeks so the goodness of the herbs is absorbed into the wine. Filter the herbs through a fine mesh sieve covered with a clean piece of muslin. Pour the wine back into its bottle, and cork.

A recipe for a red wine tonic uses approximately 2 oz (50 g) dried nettle and approximately 2 oz (50 g) of chopped apricots. Add them to $\frac{1}{2}$ pt (1 liter) of red wine and prepare as suggested. This tonic wine can be used with symptoms of tiredness and in cases of anemia to restore the blood.

inhalations

Breathing is an important way of maintaining a sense of peace and controlling panic and anxiety. Deep, steady breaths will help to restore calm. By using herbs or essentials oils with inhalations and vaporizers, the fragrances of the plants can be taken into the body. The steam will help to relax the airways and restore deeper breathing.

Use approximately two potfuls (2 pt/1 liter) of herbal tea. Pour it into a bowl. If using essential oils, place freshly boiled water in the bowl and add between three to six drops of oils. Sit comfortably, and cover your head with a large cloth or towel, so that no steam escapes. Breath the steam for about 10 minutes or until the water cools. Afterward it is important to sit in a warm room for half an hour so that the respiratory system can adjust to a normal temperature.

For an uplifting treatment use an infusion of rose petals, or several drops of rose essential oil to make an inhalation. This will help to lift the spirit and bring a sense of calm. It is also very beneficial to the complexion.

baths

A refreshing and relaxing way of experiencing the benefits of herbs is to use them in a bath. Herbal infusions or decoctions can be added to a bath. Use about 1¼ pt (600 ml) of well strained tea, adding it after the bath is filled. Essential oils can also be very effective. Add 5 drops to a bath, using less for children and the elderly. Alternatively, tie some dried herbs in a small piece of muslin or cotton and hang them on the faucet. As the bath fills the herbs will seep into the warm water.

Try an infusion of chamomile to help you relax in the evening after a day's work (see page 107). For a morning bath, use rosemary and peppermint to invigorate and refresh. A salt bath is a way of cleansing and clearing the body and aura. Add a couple of small handfuls of seasalt to a warm bath. Some lavender also works well to cleanse and soothe away cares. This has the extra benefit of relaxing tight muscles, and releasing stiffness and aches.

If a full bath is not possible, due to illness or lack of time, try a 10-minute hand or footbath. They are surprisingly effective herbal treatments. A footbath of an infusion of lavender will help restore the spirits as well as weary feet after a long day of walking or standing. Fill a small basin or bowl with a herbal tea or decoction. Add water to make it a comfortable temperature. Soak hands or feet in this bath. Dry carefully afterward.

herbal oils

Herbal oils are used externally, and are very helpful for massaging away stress and muscle strain. They are easy to prepare and inexpensive to make. They last for about a year. Herbal oils are not the same as essential oils, although some of their properties will be similar.

Use pharmaceutical olive oil which is available in glass bottles from some chemists. Pour out a small amount of oil, approximately one to two teaspoons. Add flowers or herbs. Leave this to set on a sunny windowsill for two days to three weeks, depending on the weather. When the herbs are absorbed into the oil, it may change color depending on the herbs used. When the color is even at all levels, strain out the herbs or flowers from the oil by pouring it through fine muslin or coffee filter paper. Wash the bottle and sterilize it with boiling water. Leave it to dry and refill it with the oil.

A good oil to help relieve nerve pain, or to help with the healing and scarring of burns (or sunburn) is hypericum oil. St. John's wort flowers or hypericum, should be picked when in bloom. There are red dots on the edges of the flowers which mark the presence of oil glands. Prepare the oil as suggested. It will turn a deep red as the sun draws out the hypericum. This is one oil that will last indefinitely as the hypericum acts as a preservative (see page 75).

MATERIA
MEDICA

Achillea millefolium

A relation to the dandelion and daisy, this tall-stemmed flower grows wild in fields and hedgerows.

Parts used – The whole plant is gathered in flower between June and September.

Indications – An excellent remedy to help stop bleeding, yarrow can be used externally on wounds, or internally to staunch bleeding from the nose, digestive system, or the uterus. It helps to regulate the menstrual system and is a tonic for the nervous system. It is a standard remedy to cool fevers.

Combinations – For fevers, yarrow combines well with elderflower and peppermint.

Cautions – Avoid taking during the first three months of pregnancy.

Dosages – Make a tea using 1–2 teaspoons of dried herb in one cup of boiled water and leave to infuse for 10–15 minutes. Drink three times a day or hourly for fevers. Alternatively, take 1–4 ml of tincture three times a day.

Alchemilla vulgaris

This green leafy plant, with delicate yellow flowers, holds dewdrops in its large leaves.

Parts used – The roots, leaves, and flowers can be used fresh or dried in teas.

Indications – A tonic for women's reproductive systems, it reduces period pain, regulates periods, and stops excessive bleeding. It can be used after childbirth, abortion, and miscarriage to support the uterus. The fresh root is good for treating diarrhea and gastroenteritis.

Cautions – Avoid during pregnancy.

Dosages – Make a tea using 2 teaspoons of dried herb in a cup of boiled water and infuse for 10–15 minutes. For diarrhea, make a decoction by boiling 1 teaspoon of the root for 10 minutes in one cup of water. Drink three times a day. Alternatively, take 2–4 ml of tincture three times a day.

Allium sativum

This herb is known for its delicious taste and powerful healing properties.

Parts used – Garlic cloves are part of the bulb of the plant.

Indications – This powerful herb is antimicrobial, fighting against bacteria, viruses, and parasites. It can be used for sore throats, coughs, colds, flu, and gastric infections. It helps re-establish bacterial flora in the gut after the use of antibiotics. It is a useful remedy for clearing fevers and catarrh. If taken over a long period of time, it helps to reduce blood pressure and blood cholesterol levels. Externally, it can be used on verucas and in an oil for ear infections.

Combinations – Combines well with echinacea to fight infections.

Cautions – Use with care during breast-feeding as this herb may upset the baby's digestion.

Dosages – Eat a clove three times a day, in cooking or raw in salad.

Aloe vera

This fleshy-leaved succulent, originally from Africa, is now commonly grown as a houseplant.

Parts used – The leaves contain a healing gel that is an excellent remedy for irritated skin. "Bitter aloes" is derived from the plant's skin. This is very strong and can act as a laxative.

Indications – Externally, this cooling, healing gel soothes skin irritations caused by burns, sunburn, and allergic reactions. Applied to hemorrhoids, it soothes pain and speeds healing. Internally, it soothes and protects the digestive system, helping with colitis, irritable bowel syndrome, and ulcers.

Combinations – Aloe juice, taken internally, may need ginger or turmeric to stop griping pains, as it is a strong laxative.

Cautions – Stimulates the uterus, so avoid taking it internally during pregnancy, while breast-feeding, or during heavy periods. Also avoid taking internally if there is a history of kidney disease.

Dosages – The fleshy parts of the leaves can be split to obtain a clear gel that can be applied to the skin twice daily. Internally take 0.1–0.3 grams of juice, but seek professional guidance.

Althaea officinalis

These tall, attractive flowering plants grow well in salt marshes and damp, fertile places.

Parts used – The leaves can be picked in summer after flowering. The root is dug up in the autumn.

Indications – Digestive, respiratory, and urinary inflammations – such as ulcers, indigestion, dry irritating coughs, and cystitis – are all helped by this herb. Externally, it can be applied to wasp and bee stings, scalds, burns, and skin rashes.

Cautions – This herb may slow the absorption of medications.

Dosages – A decoction can be made using one teaspoon of chopped root simmered gently in one cup of water for 10 minutes. Make a tea using 1–2 teaspoons of dried leaves and infuse for 10–15 minutes. Drink three times a day. Alternatively, take 1–4 ml of tincture three times a day. This herb makes a valuable compress or poultice.

Anethum graveolens

This aromatic Mediterranean herb has flat yellow-green flowers that carry the sweet scent of aniseed.

Parts used – Collect the seeds when they are fully ripe and have turned brown.

Indications – An excellent remedy for the digestion, dill relieves flatulence and griping pains, and is safe to use with children. It stimulates the milk flow in nursing mothers. It is a gentle, soothing remedy that aids relaxation and brings a good night's sleep.

Dosages – Use 1–2 teaspoons of crushed seed with one cup of water to make a tea. Delicious with added honey. For wind and colic, take tea before meals. Alternatively, use 1–2 ml of tincture three times a day.

Artemisia vulgaris

This tall, downy-leaved plant grows wild on hedgebanks and roadsides.

Parts used – The leaves and the root are collected and dried.

Indications – Mugwort has stimulating and tonifying properties, which are especially effective for regulating the menstrual cycle and increasing fertility. It is stimulating to the digestive system through its bitter taste. Used in Chinese medicine as moxibustion treatment, it warms and strengthens certain areas of the body and the acupuncture points.

Dosages – Make a tea using 1–2 teaspoons of dried herb in one cup of boiled water and leave to infuse for 10–15 minutes. Drink three times a day. Alternatively, take 1–4 ml of tincture three times a day. A sprig of mugwort can also be used to flavor an aperitif.

Avena sativa

The common oat is used in porridge for a hearty breakfast.

Parts used – The seeds and whole plant are used. It is harvested in the late summer.

Indications – Oats are one of the best remedies for nourishing and supporting the nervous system. They are very useful for recovery from nervous exhaustion. Oats are also good for general debility, and as tonic for children who are weak and underweight.

Dosages – Oats are mostly taken as porridge. Alternatively, take 3–5 ml of fluid extract three times a day.

Borago officinalis

This hardy plant, with its bright blue flowers, is attractive to bees.

Parts used – Gather the leaves in early summer, just before they come into flower. Use the flowers for decorations. Dried leaves can be used for making teas.

Indications – A tonic that repairs adrenal glands affected by stress and steroid medications. A cooling and cleansing herb, good for detoxifying the body, helpful for clearing boils, skin rashes, and infections. Strengthening for convalescence, especially after respiratory illnesses.

Dosages – Pour one cup of water on 2 teaspoonfuls of dried herb. Infuse for 10–15 minutes, then drink three times a day. Alternatively, take 1–4ml of tincture three times a day.

Calendula officinalis

These yellow flowers brighten gardens, celebrating the summer sunshine.

Parts used – The yellow petals can be collected between June and September.

Indications – Marigold is effective for fighting infections due to bacteria, viruses, fungus, and parasites. It clears lymphatic congestion and has a healing effect on gastric complaints. It helps to regulate menstruation. It has a reputation for treating tumors and cysts in the reproductive system. Externally it is a soothing remedy for eczema and other irritated skin conditions.

Combinations – Marigold combines well with cleavers as a lymphatic cleanser.

Cautions – Avoid taking internally when pregnant.

Dosages – Make tea using 1–2 teaspoons of dried herb in one cup of boiled water: infuse for 10–15 minutes. Drink three times a day. Alternatively, take 1–4 ml of tincture three times a day.

Chamaemelum nobilis, Matricaria chamomilla syn. recutita

These delicate, daisylike flowers create a relaxing presence and fragrance in any garden.

Parts used – Gather the flowers between May and August when they are not too wet or damp. Dry with care. The temperature should not be too high.

Indications – A relaxing remedy that relieves stress and tension. It works well on the digestive system, clearing wind and gastric pains. It is also good for inflammations, such as sore throats.

Combinations – Combines well with lemon balm and linden flowers for a relaxing tea.

Dosages – Use 2 teaspoons of dried flowers per cup of boiling water to make an infusion and leave to infuse for 5–10 minutes. For a herbal bath, make a strong infusion of half a cup of flowers with $3\frac{1}{2}$ pt (2 liters) of boiling water. Let it sit for 10 minutes and strain into bath.

Cimicifuga racemosa

A beautiful plant that is native to the shady woods of Canada and North America.

Parts used – The roots are unearthed in the autumn after the fruits have ripened. They need to be split lengthwise and dried carefully.

Indications – Balances the hormones, especially during menopause, relieving hot flushes, depression, and low libido. It eases painful periods, labor pains, neuralgia, sciatica, and arthritic aches.

Combinations – For menopausal complaints, combine with wild yam. Add motherwort to help with excessive bleeding and hot flushes. Add skullcap, vervain, and wild oats if nervous or depressed. For palpitations, add motherwort, hawthorn, and lemon balm.

Cautions – Do not use during pregnancy, and only under guidance during childbirth.

Dosages – For a decoction, simmer one cup of water with $\frac{1}{2}$ to 1 teaspoon of dried root for 10–15 minutes. Take three times a day. Alternatively, take 2–4 ml of tincture three times a day.

Crataegus oxyacanthoides

These beautiful red berries brighten the day and heal the heart.

Parts used – The berries can be collected in September and October.

Indications – This gentle remedy is excellent for the heart and circulatory system, stimulating or depressing the heart activity and normalizing its functions. It can be used as a long-term treatment for palpitations, heart failure or weakness, high blood pressure, arteriosclerosis, and angina.

Combinations – For treatment of arteriosclerosis, combine with linden flower.

Dosages – Pour a cup of boiled water on 2 teaspoons of berries and infuse for 20 minutes. Drink three times a day for a long period of time. Alternatively, take 2–4 ml of tincture three times a day.

Dioscorea villosa

This tropical plant is widely grown in western parts of Africa.

Parts used – The roots are collected in the autumn.

Indications – A valuable herb used to relieve spasm in the colon, it helps relieve irritable bowel syndrome and colic. It also soothes period cramps and ovarian pain.

Combinations – For intestinal colic, combine wild yam with chamomile.

Dosages – Make a decoction using 1–2 teaspoons of herb in a cup of water. Simmer gently for 10–15 minutes. Drink three times a day. Alternatively, take 2–4 ml of tincture three times a day.

Echinacea angustifolia or *purpurea*

A beautiful, pinky-purple flower with daisylike petals and a dark, conical center.

Parts used – The roots can be collected in the autumn and dried.

Indications – Echinacea has an important role to play in fighting viruses and bacteria. It is therefore useful for colds, flu, tonsillitis, and laryngitis, as well as boils and skin infections. It is helpful in preventing recurring infections through its support to the immune system.

Combinations – This herb can be combined with many different herbs to help clear infections.

Dosages – Make a decoction using 1–2 teaspoons of the root with one cup of water. Simmer for 10–15 minutes and drink twice a day. Alternatively, take 1–4ml of tincture twice a day.

Equisetum arvense

These tall rushes, with their characteristic bristly fronds, grow in marshy areas.

Parts used – Horsetail stems are collected in early summer and dried in bunches, but are more readily bought through herbal suppliers.

Indications – Horsetail is toning and astringing to the urinary system, helping with bed-wetting in children and with incontinence. It has a high silica content, so is good for the nails and hair. It stops bleeding both internal and externally, and is a good wound healer. It is useful for treating benign enlarged prostrate glands.

Dosages – Use one cup of boiled water on 2 teaspoons of the dried plant and infuse for 15–20 minutes. Drink three times a day. Alternatively, take 2–4 ml of tincture three times a day.

Filipendula ulmaria

With its sweet scent and pretty blossom, this plant deserves its country name "lady of the meadows."

Parts used – The open flowers and leaves can be picked during flowering between June and August.

Indications – Meadowsweet offers pain relief and anti-inflammatory action for hot, swollen joints, headaches, and neuralgia. It brings relaxation and induces peaceful sleep. One of the best remedies for the digestion, it protects and soothes the mucous membranes of the digestive tract, helping with heartburn, diarrhea, and ulcers. It also brings out fevers, and so clears rashes, colds, and flu.

Dosages – Make a tea using 1–2 teaspoons of dried herb in one cup of boiled water and leave to infuse for 10–15 minutes. Drink three times a day. Alternatively, take 1–4 ml of tincture three times a day.

Flos chrysanthemi morifolii

The finest quality yellow chryanthemums come from the city of Hangzhou in China, and are known as hang juhua.

Parts used – The flowers are gathered when they are at their height of bloom in the autumn.

Indications – Chrysanthemums help to clear fevers and the headaches of colds and flu. They strengthen the eyes, helping reduce redness, tearing, and sensitivity to light. Their calming properties relieve tension headaches, dizziness, and vertigo.

Combinations – For dizziness and blurred vision due to weakness, combine with *gou qi zi*.

Cautions – Use with caution if there is poor appetite or diarrhea. Use the Chinese chrysanthemums as a herb.

Dosages – For a decoction, simmer 5–10 grams of dried flowers with three cups of water for 10 minutes. Drink over one day. Alternatively, take 2–5 ml of tincture three times a day.

Fructus lycii

This sweet orange berry is also known as lycium fruit, matrimony vine fruit, or Chinese wolfberry fruit.

Parts used – The fruit is harvested in the summer or autumn when ripe.

Indications – A gentle tonic that strengthens the liver and kidneys, as well as nourishing the blood. It nourishes the eyes, so it is good for weak eyesight and blurred vision. As a remedy for old age, it helps backache, weak legs, and general tiredness.

Combinations – For tinnitus, headache, and poor eyesight due to weakness, combine *gou qi zi* and ju hua. As a tonic combine with *gan cao*.

Cautions – Avoid eating if the digestion is weak and there are loose stools.

Dosages – For a decoction, use 10 grams of dried fruit with three cups of water. Simmer gently for 20 minutes. Drink over the course of the day. Alternatively, take 2–5 ml of tincture three times a day. The fruit can be baked into bread or eaten on its own.

Fructus schisandrae Chinensis

This shiny red berry has a most unusual taste.

Parts used – The fruit is harvested in the autumn when ripe.

Indications – This Chinese tonic builds up the *qi*, or energy, in the kidneys and lungs. It helps to stop night sweats. Quieting and calming, it helps promote a deep sleep and relieves palpitations. Its traditional use was as a sex tonic for men and women.

Cautions – This fruit may cause heartburn.

Dosages – For a decoction, use 3–10 grams of dried fruit with three cups of water. Simmer gently for 30 minutes. Drink over the course of the day. Alternatively, take 2–5 ml of tincture three times a day.

Galium aparine

A common weed with long, thin stems and tiny prickles that catch onto anything that brushes past.

Parts used – Gather leaves and stems before flowering.

Indications – A very valuable plant, cleavers is one of the best tonics for the lymphatic system and is good for tonsillitis and swollen glands. It is also useful for the treatment of cystitis and other urinary conditions.

Combinations – Combine with echinacea and marigold to make a good lymphatic cleanser.

Dosages – Pour a cup of boiling water on 2–3 teaspoons of the dried herb to make an infusion. Drink three cups a day. Or take 2–4 ml of tincture three times a day.

Gingko biloba

One of the most ancient species of tree, known to have survived the last ice age in China.

Parts used – The leaves and seeds are used.

Indications – Gingko encourages good circulation, especially to the brain, aiding memory and concentration. Recent research suggests it is useful for senile dementia. It is helpful for some cases of asthma, especially in children.

Cautions – Consult a herbal or medical practitioner if you are taking medication for a circulatory-related condition.

Dosages – Use one teaspoon of dried herb with a cup of boiling water to make an infusion. Drink two cups a day. Take 2–4ml of tincture twice daily. Tablets are available commercially.

Glycyrrhiza glabra

There are may varieties of this sweet root, which is native to southern Europe and Asia.

Parts used – The root is dug up in early autumn and dried.

Indications – Licorice root has a beneficial effect on the endocrine system, strengthening the adrenal glands. It eases coughs and helps to clear the chest, making it an important ingredient in cough and asthma mixtures. It is helpful to the digestion, protecting the liver and healing ulcers.

Cautions – Do not take licorice if suffering from high blood pressure. Avoid during pregnancy.

Dosages – Make a decoction using ½–1 teaspoon of root in a cup of water. Simmer for 10–15 minutes. Drink three times a day. Alternatively, take 1–3 ml of tincture three times a day.

Granum floris pollinis

These small orange grains are the pollens of wild flowers.

Parts used – Flower pollen collected by bees.

Indications – This unique remedy is nourishing and restoring to all parts of the body. It contains many essential nutrients, which repair and rejuvenate the organs and tissues. It stimulates the immune system and reduces allergic reactions.

Cautions – Although this remedy can be used to treat allergic reactions, it can sometimes cause them. To be safe, start with a small dose, 1/4 teaspoon daily, then increase to normal dose if there is no reaction.

Dosages – One teaspoon a day on an empty stomach.

Humulus lupulus

This fast-growing vine has been an ingredient in medicinal brews for centuries.

Parts used – Hops are gathered before they are ripe in late summer and dried in the shade.

Indications – Hops is an excellent remedy to help calm the nervous system, relieving stress and tension. It helps most symptoms of stress, such as tension headaches, restlessness, and insomnia.

Combinations – Hops combines well with valerian and passiflora for insomnia.

Cautions – Do not use hops if there are signs of depression.

Dosages – Use 1 teaspoon of dried flowers per cup of boiled water to make a tea. Drink at night to help you fall asleep. alternatively, take 1–4ml of tincture before bedtime.

Hydrastis canadensis

This potent herb comes in the form of a fine yellow powder.

Parts used – The root is dried and powdered. This plant is protected and it is illegal to gather it.

Indications – This useful herb helps treat gastric and respiratory conditions such as ulcers, colitis, and chest infections. It helps stop excessive menstrual bleeding and stimulates the uterus during childbirth. Externally, it fights infections, healing earaches, conjunctivitis, and ringworm.

Combinations – For gastric conditions, golden seal combines well with meadowsweet and chamomile. To clear catarrhal infections, combine with hyssop and echinacea.

Cautions – Avoid during pregnancy as this herb may stimulate the muscles of the uterus. Avoid if you have high blood pressure.

Dosages – Use a half teaspoon of powdered herb in a cup of boiled water to drink as a tea. Alternatively, take in capsules, or 2–4ml of tincture three times a day. Do not exceed dosage.

Hypericum perforatum

This golden flower grows wild in woodlands, but is also a beautiful addition to the garden.

Parts used – The leaves, stem, and flowers can be gathered when in flower.

Indications – St John's wort helps with anxiety and depression. It is useful during the menopause to calm irritability and tension. It heals neuralgic pain. Externally, an oil or lotion made with St. John's wort heals wounds and bruises, varicose veins, and burns. It is useful after strokes to restore sensation to the limbs.

Cautions – Avoid taking this herb if on anti-depressants, digoxin, theophylline, the contraceptive pill, or medication for migraine or epilepsy. If you are currently taking St. John's wort *and* prescribed medication, tell your pharmacist and doctor. Avoid if pregnant and do not give to children.

Dosages – Make a tea using 1–2 teaspoons of dried herb in one cup of boiled water. Leave to infuse 10–15 minutes. Drink three times a day. Alternatively, take 1–4 ml of tincture three times a day.

Lavendula officinalis

A heavenly, scented flower used in soaps, cosmetics, and perfumes.

Parts used – The flowers are best collected in June and September before opening.

Indications – This herb is harmonizing to the nervous system, balancing moods and emotions. It lifts depression, calms anxiety and promotes natural sleep.

Combinations – For depression, combine with skullcap and rosemary. For headaches, use with valerian.

Dosages – Make a tea using 1 teaspoon of dried herb in one cup of boiled water and leave to infuse for 10 minutes. Drink three times a day. Also delicious added to soups, stews, and desserts. Use lavender oil in the bath, or make a strong infusion using ½ cup of flowers in 2 pints (1 liter) of water and add this to the bath.

Leonurus cardiaca

This tall plant with hairy leaves and clusters of pink flowers grows on wasteland and in hedgerows.

Parts used – Gather the flowers and leaves during flowering between June and September.

Indications – Motherwort is a valuable herb for treating delayed or suppressed menstruation. It is a relaxing herb for menopausal complaints, helping to calm anxiety and stop palpitations. It is a strengthening tonic for the heart, useful for an over-rapid heartbeat, and other conditions affected by stress and anxiety.

Combinations – Combine motherwort with hawthorn berries to treat palpitations and other heart conditions associated with anxiety and tension. It combines well with other herbs to treat menopausal complaints, depending on what is needed.

Cautions – Avoid using during the first three months of pregnancy.

Dosages – Make a tea using 1–2 teaspoons of dried herb in one cup of boiled water and leave to infuse for 10–15 minutes. Drink three times a day. Alternatively, take 1–4 ml of tincture three times a day.

Melaleuca alternifolia

This heavily scented plant grows throughout the South Pacific.

Parts used – The leaves and buds are gathered for herbal use.

Indications – This herb is mainly used externally as an inhalation, mouthwash, or aromatherapy oil. It fights bacterial, fungal, and viral infections on the skin and in the mouth and lungs. When combined with massage, it eases varicose veins by moving blood stagnation. Stimulating to the nerves, it promotes clear thinking and relieves depression.

Dosages – Use 1–3 drops of essential oil in a steam inhalation to clear chest infections. For skin infections or fungal conditions, use 1–3 drops of essential oil in water or a base oil on affected area.

Melissa officinalis

This common flowering plant, with its lemon-scented leaves, is another that is loved by bees.

Parts used – The leaves can be picked and used fresh in a tea.

Indications – A strengthening herb for the nervous system, it is good for calming stressful states, and clearing sorrows. It helps with depression, palpitations, and headaches. Particularly good during the menopause, it also relieves hot flushes and regulates periods. It helps fight infections, and eases viral symptoms of colds, flu, shingles, and cold sores.

Combinations – Combine with linden flower for a refreshing and relaxing summer drink.

Dosages – Make a tea using 1–2 teaspoons of fresh or dried herb in one cup of boiled water and leave to infuse for 10–15 minutes. Drink three times a day. Alternatively take 2–6 ml of the tincture three times a day.

Mentha piperita

This minty herb cools and refreshes, but will overtake the garden with its robust growth.

Parts used – The leaves and stems are gathered just before the flowers open.

Indications – An excellent remedy for digestive complaints such as wind and colic, it stimulates the digestive juices and relaxes the intestines. It stops nausea and vomiting, so it can be useful for travel sickness. Fevers, colds, and flu are eased by drinking this herbal tea. As a nerve tonic it helps soothe anxiety and tensions.

Combinations – For colds and flu, combine peppermint with elderflower and hyssop.

Dosages – Make a tea using 1–2 teaspoons of dried or fresh herb in one cup of boiled water and leave to infuse for 10–15 minutes. Drink as often as desired. Alternatively, take 1–2 ml of tincture three times a day.

Nepeta cataria

This cottage garden plant, with silvery green leaves and small mauve flowers, is loved by cats!

Parts used – The leaves and flowers are collected between June and September.

Indications – A traditional cold and flu remedy, it is very good at fighting off feverish conditions. Generally very relaxing, it is a gentle, safe herb that can be used with children.

Combinations – Combine with elderflower and yarrow to treat colds. For a relaxing summer drink, combine with lemon balm.

Dosages – Use 2 teaspoons of dried herb per cup of boiling water for an infusion. Infuse for 10–15 minutes and drink three times a day. Alternatively, take 2–4 ml of tincture three times a day.

Ocimum basilicum

A fragrant green plant often used in cooking and salads.

Parts used – Delicate stems and leaves can be used fresh or dried.

Indications – A cleansing remedy for infections, it clears phlegm from the nose and chest. Its anti-spasmodic effect helps to relax the digestion, easing wind, nausea and stomach cramps. It relieves travel sickness. Basil strengthens the nerves and releases tensions, improving clarity of thought and concentration.

Combinations – Take as a hot tea with honey to promote clarity of mind.

Cautions – Do not use during pregnancy.

Dosages – Use one teaspoon of dried herb, or two teaspoons of the fresh plant with a cup of boiling water to make an infusion. Drink two cups a day.

Origanum vulgare

This low-growing Mediterranean herb is fragrant and rich in taste.

Parts used – The leaves and stems can be chopped and used in teas or in cooking.

Indications – Sweet marjoram has a long history of herbal use, good for warding off infections, clearing phlegm, and soothing coughs and fevers. Its warming properties help the digestion, one reason it is often used in cooking. Its warmth also relaxes and relieves mental and physical tensions. The oil massaged into joints eases stiff and painful muscles.

Caution – Avoid using during pregnancy.

Dosages – Make a tea using 1 teaspoon of dried herb in a cup of boiled water and leave to infuse for 10–15 minutes. Drink three times a day. Or take 2ml of tincture three times a day. Delicious added to stew and soups.

Passiflora incarnata

An unusual and beautiful flower that grows well in a warm, sunny courtyard.

Parts used – The leaves can be collected before the flowers bloom, between May and July, or while there is fruit on the vine.

Indications – A wonderfully relaxing remedy that helps with sleep difficulties, whether due to overwork or exhaustion. It relaxes spasms so it is good for seizures, Parkinson's disease, or hysteria. It is beneficial for the nervous system, relieving stress and tension.

Combinations – For insomnia, combine passiflora with valerian and hops.

Dosages – Make a tea using one teaspoon of dried herb and leave to infuse for 15 minutes. Drink one cup in the evening for sleeplessness or twice a day for other conditions. Alternatively, take 1–4 ml of tincture in the same way as the dried herb.

Pericarpium citri reticulatae

The bitter, aromatic taste of the tangerine peel encourages good digestion.

Parts used – The dried peel is used.

Indications – This herb encourages good digestion, treating bloating, belching, nausea, and fullness in the abdomen. It moves the *qi*, or energy, helping fatigue, loss of appetite, and stifling sensations in the chest.

Combinations – Used with tonic herbs such as *huang qi*, it helps to prevent bloating.

Cautions – Avoid with fevers and coughs.

Dosages – For a decoction use 3–9 grams of dried peel with three cups of water, simmer gently for 30 minutes. Drink after meals. Alternatively, take 2 ml of tincture three times a day.

Radix angelicae sinensis

Chinese angelica is a famous blood tonic that is warming and nourishing.

Parts used – The root is gathered and dried.

Indications – *Dang gui* nourishes the blood and encourages circulation. Excellent for menstrual problems, it regulates periods and eases cramping pains and premenstrual symptoms. It helps with anemia and poor circulation. Moistening to the intestines, it helps relieve constipation due to dryness.

Combinations – For exhaustion after childbirth, combine with *huang qi*.

Cautions – Do not take if pregnant or trying to conceive.

Dosages – For a decoction, use 3–15 grams of dried root with three cups of water, simmer gently for 30–45 minutes. Drink over the course of the day. Alternatively, take 2–5 ml of tincture three times a day.

Radix astragali membranacei

This Chinese herb was first mentioned in the *Shen Nong Ben Cao* written in the first century A.D.

Parts used – The roots are harvested in the spring or autumn when the plants are more than four years old.

Indications – This tonic herb strengthens the *qi*, or energy, helping with tiredness and weakness. It enhances the immune system, useful for frequent colds and flu. In the treatment of cancer and AIDS, it helps to protect against viruses and infections. It helps control excessive sweating due to debility, and promotes the healing of skin ulcers.

Combinations – For tiredness and poor circulation, it combines well with *dang gui*. This combination also helps recovery from childbirth.

Dosages – For a decoction, use 10 grams of dried root with three cups of water. Simmer gently for 45 minutes. Drink over the course of the day. Alternatively, take 5 ml of tincture three times a day.

Radix ginseng

This valuable Chinese herb has been used for centuries as a tonic.

Parts used – The root is cultivated in China, Korea, and North America.

Indications – Ginseng is a strong tonic, aiding the digestion and general well-being. It is very strengthening for the elderly, or after a long illness. It clears shock, and increases resistance to stress. By increasing white blood cells, it supports the immune system and helps with anti-cancer treatments. It is a useful herb for treating depression caused by exhaustion and debility.

Combinations – Ginseng is found in many Chinese herbal tonic prescriptions.

Cautions – Only use if there are signs of weakness. Avoid during pregnancy. Avoid during acute inflammatory conditions and infections as it may aggravate symptoms.

Dosages – For a decoction, use 3–9 grams of dried root with three cups of water. Simmer gently for 45 minutes. Drink over the course of the day. Alternatively, take 5 ml of tincture in a small amount of water. Take for up to two months, then rest before resuming.

Radix glycyrrhizae uralensis

This sweet herb plays a large role in Chinese herbal treatments. It is also known as Chinese licorice root.

Parts used – The root is sliced and dried.

Indications – This herb is a tonic to the digestive system, strengthening and toning its functions. It builds up the *qi*, or energy, and is useful with tiredness, shortness of breath, and weakness. Moistening to the lungs, it soothes coughs. It relieves spasms and is useful for cramping in the abdomen and legs.

Combinations – This herb combines well with many other herbs and is widely used in many traditional prescriptions.

Cautions – Avoid taking *gan cao* if you have high blood pressure.

Dosages – For a decoction, use 5 grams of dried root with three cups of water, simmer gently for 45 minutes. Drink over the course of the day. Alternatively, take 2–5 ml of tincture three times a day.

Radix panacis quinquefolii

American ginseng grows in the mountains of Canada and northern USA.

Parts used – The roots are gathered and dried.

Indications – Similar to Chinese ginseng, this root is strengthening and healing. Although it is not as strong as Chinese ginseng, it is more cooling and replenishing to the *yin*. Used after a high fever, when there are signs of debility, thirst, and irritability, it nourishes the vital essences within the body. Traditionally it has been used in the treatment of tuberculosis.

Dosages – For a decoction, use 3–9 grams of dried root with three cups of water. Simmer gently for 45 minutes. Drink over the course of the day. As a tincture, take 2–5 ml three times a day.

Ramulus cinnamomi cassiae

Delicious spicy cinnamon adds flavor and warmth to cooking and drinks.

Parts used – The twigs and bark are used.

Indications – *Gui zhi* warms and encourages circulation. It is good for stiff joints and pains that are worse in cold weather. It helps facilitate menstrual bleeding and eases cramping pains. Good for the heart, it relieves chest pains and palpitations.

Cautions – Avoid with ongoing fever, or signs of heat. Use with caution during pregnancy and with excessive menstrual bleeding.

Dosages – For a decoction, use 3–9 grams of dried herb with three cups of water. Simmer gently for 30 minutes. Drink over the course of the day. Alternatively, add to other teas for a warming effect. Cinnamon is also good in cakes, cookies, and curries.

Rosa spp.

The beauty of the rose gives joy through its scent, color, and form.

Parts used – The flower petals can be picked when they have lost moisture and rose hips can be gathered in the autumn.

Indications – Rose has an uplifting and restoring effect upon the nerves. It is calming and soothing, easing depression, irritability, grief, and anger. It heals heartache, helping those who feel a lack of love in their lives. For the female reproductive system, this herb eases pain and heavy periods. It relieves premenstrual tension and difficult emotions during the menopause. It enhances sexual feelings, and treats problems with conception, such as infertility and impotence.

Cautions – Rose can stimulate the uterus, so avoid during pregnancy.

Dosages – Make a tea using 1–2 teaspoons of dried herb and leave to infuse for 10–15 minutes. Drink three times a day. Alternatively, take 1–4 ml of tincture three times a day.

Rosmarinus officinalis

This aromatic herb is well-known for its flavor.

Parts used – The leaves can be gathered throughout the summer, but are best during flowering.

Indications – Rosemary stimulates the nervous and circulatory systems, toning and calming the digestion. Headaches, indigestion, and depression associated with debility can be helped by this herb. Externally, it may be used to ease muscular pain, sciatica, and neuralgia.

Combinations – For depression, combine rosemary with skullcap and wild oats.

Cautions – Avoid use during pregnancy. Avoid if you have high blood pressure.

Dosages – Make a tea using 1–2 teaspoons of dried herb in one cup of boiled water and leave to infuse for 10–15 minutes. Drink three times a day. Alternatively, take 1–2 ml of tincture three times a day.

Salvia officinalis

This aromatic plant brings beauty to the garden with its gray-green leaves and purple flowers.

Parts used – The leaves can be used any time, but are best collected in dry, sunny weather in May and June before the plant flowers.

Indications – Sage is useful for inflammations of the mouth and throat, such as mouth ulcers, gingivitis, and sore throats.

Combinations – Excellent for hot flushes and sweating, it combines well with other herbs for the menopause. Burning dried sage or sage oil helps to cleanse and clear negativity in the house.

Cautions – Avoid during pregnancy as it stimulates the uterus, and when breast-feeding.

Dosages – Make a tea using 1–2 teaspoons of dried herb and leave to infuse for 10 minutes. Drink three times a day. Alternatively, take 1–4 ml of tincture three times a day. For a mouthwash, make a stronger tea using 2 teaspoons of leaves. Gargle with the hot tea several times a day.

Sambucus nigra

The elder tree is a "medicine chest of herbs", each part of the tree offering healing.

Parts used – The flowers and leaves are gathered in spring and early summer. The berries are collected in August and September.

Indications – The flowers make a delicious tea, useful for treating colds and flu, especially if taken at their onset. They are a good treatment for cattarhal conditions such as sinusitis, hay fever and glue ear. They relax and soothe the nerves, and are particularly useful as a night-time drink that gives restful sleep. The leaves are used externally to help clear bruises, sprains, and chilblains.

Combinations – For colds and fevers, combine with peppermint, yarrow, and hyssop.

Dosages – For an infusion, use 2 teaspoons of the dried or fresh flower to one cup of boiling water. Infuse for 10 minutes. The leaves can be made into a poultice, compress or ointment and used externally. The berries can be simmered for several minutes in water and taken with honey.

Scutellaria laterifolia

The blue flowers of skullcap are followed by seed pods shaped like a cap, giving this plant its name.

Parts used – The stems, leaves, and flowers are used, and can be collected late in the flowering period in August and September.

Indications – A good nerve tonic, skullcap helps to relax and strengthen the nervous system. It treats epilepsy, seizures, and hysteria, and can be used in exhausted or depressed states. It is very helpful with premenstrual tension and headaches caused by stress.

Combinations – Combines with valerian and other nervine tonics to ease stress and anxiety.

Dosages – Make a tea using 1–2 teaspoons of dried herb and leave to infuse for 10–15 minutes. Drink three times a day. Alternatively, take 2–4 ml of tincture three times a day.

Semen coicis lachryma – jobi

This large, round, white seed is similar to barley in its actions and nature.

Parts used – The seeds are harvested in the autumn when ripened.

Indications – This gentle herb is an effective treatment for promoting urination, thus clearing edema and swelling due to water retention. It is strengthening to the digestion, stopping diarrhea and loose stools.

Cautions – Use with care during pregnancy.

Dosages – For a decoction, use 10–20 grams of dried herb with three cups of water. Simmer gently for 30 minutes. Drink over the course of the day. Alternatively, take 5 ml of tincture three times a day. It can be taken safely over a long period of time.

Serenoa serrulata

This impressive palm bears deep red-brown berries.

Parts used – The berries are gathered from September through to July.

Indications – Saw palmetto berries tone and strengthen the male reproductive system. They can safely be used to boost male sex hormones, and are especially helpful in treatment of benign enlarged prostrate gland.

Combinations – Combine with damiana leaves to strengthen male hormones.

Dosages – Make a decoction using ½–1 teaspoon of berries in a cup of water. Simmer gently for five minutes. Drink three times a day. Alternatively, take 1–2 ml of tincture three times a day.

Stellaria media

A common garden weed with tiny, white, starlike flowers.

Parts used – Collect leaves, stems, and flowers all year long, but it is less abundant in winter.

Indications – This cooling, soothing remedy works externally to heal skin complaints such as eczema, heat rashes, and burns. Internally, it calms gastritis, indigestion, and irritable bowel syndrome. Also good as a diuretic, it can be used to treat water retention and swollen joints.

Combinations – It makes an excellent ointment when combined with marshmallow.

Dosages – Use two teaspoons of herb with one cup of boiling water to make an infusion. Infuse for 5 minutes. Drink three times a day. To relieve itching, make a strong infusion and add to bath water.

Taraxacum officinale

This well-known golden flower has a long history of herbal use.

Parts used – Leaves can be eaten in salads or used in medicinal teas. They can be collected at any time of year. Roots are best collected between June and August when they are most bitter.

Indications – Dandelion is a gentle detoxifier, ridding the body of toxins and wastes through the liver and kidneys. It supports the liver in its work as a blood cleanser and increases the production of bile, which helps the digestion. Dandelion is a powerful diuretic, high in natural sources of potassium, which is often lost with increased urination. It is good for treating water retention and arthritic conditions, as well as helping to release repressed emotions.

Combinations – To clear water retention, use with yarrow.

Dosages – Put 2–3 teaspoons of root into one cup of water, bring to a boil, and simmer for 10–15 minutes. Drink three times a day. Alternatively, use 5–10 ml of tincture three times a day.

Thymus vulgaris

This strongly scented herb is attractive to bees, and makes an excellent honey.

Parts used – The leaves and flowers can be used throughout its growing season, but are best collected for drying in the summer.

Indications – Like most herbs used in cooking, thyme helps the digestion of food. It is also highly antiseptic and anti-microbial and therefore good for coughs and colds, sore throats, and tonsillitis. Externally, it can be used on cuts and wounds. Warming and exhilarating to the circulation, it is a tonic for physical and mental exhaustion and depression.

Dosages – Make a tea using 2 teaspoons of dried herb and leave to infuse for 10 minutes. Drink three times a day. Alternatively, take 2–4 ml of tincture three times a day. Use in cooking.

Tilia europaea

These magnificent trees, with their sweet-scented blossoms, often line pathways through parks in Europe.

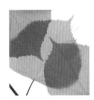

Parts used – The flowers are collected in midsummer and dried in the shade.

Indications – Linden flower is a relaxing remedy for nervous tension, calming excitable children and aiding sleep. Beneficial for the circulation, it helps with raised blood pressure caused by arteriosclerosis and tension. An excellent cold remedy, it clears fevers and restlessness.

Combinations – Combine with hawthorn berries to treat raised blood pressure, with hops and lemon balm to soothe nervous tension, and with elderflower to clear the common cold.

Cautions – This herb can bring on hot flushes during the menopause.

Dosages – Make a tea using 1 teaspoon of dried herb in one cup of boiled water. Leave to infuse for 10 minutes. Drink three times a day. Alternatively, take 1–2 ml of tincture three times a day.

Trifolium pratense

These pink and white honey-scented blossoms grow in fields and meadows.

Parts used – The flowers can be gathered between May and September.

Indications – This gentle herbal remedy is effective for children's skin complaints such as eczema and psoriasis. Its relaxant properties help to relieve stress-related complaints of headaches, muscle tension, and hyperactivity. Recent research suggests it is effective as an anti-cancer remedy for the breasts and ovaries.

Combinations – For skin conditions combine, red clover with yellow dock and nettles.

Dosages – Make a tea using 1–3 teaspoons of dried herb and leave to infuse for 10–15 minutes. Drink three times a day. Alternatively, take 2–6 ml of tincture three times a day.

Tuber ophiopogonis japonici

These soft, sweet, fleshy roots are yellowish-white in color.

Parts used – The roots are gathered and dried.

Indications – *Mai men dong* nourishes fluids in the lung and stomach. It is an effective treatment for dry coughs, thirst, and constipation. Calming to the heart, it soothes irritability and agitation, especially if these conditions have worsened in the evening or at night.

Combinations – For weakness and irritability due to excessive sweating, combine with *huang qi* and *wu wei zi*.

Cautions – Do not use if there are signs of diarrhea.

Dosages – For a decoction, use 6–15 grams of dried root with three cups of water. Simmer gently for 30 minutes. Drink over the course of the day. Alternatively, take 2–5 ml of tincture three times a day.

Turnera aphrodisiaca

This subtropical herb brings its warmth to strengthen and nourish the body.

Parts used – The leaves and stems are gathered at the time of flowering.

Indications – An excellent nerve tonic, damiana also has an long-standing reputation as an aphrodisiac, and supports the reproductive system. It can be especially helpful for male reproductive problems.

Combinations – As a nerve tonic, it is often combined with oats. Combine with saw palmetto berries for male reproductive problems. Use with agnus castus for irregular periods and menopausal symptoms, especially if these are accompanied by fatigue and depression.

Cautions – Only use with signs of fatigue.

Dosages – Pour a cup of boiling water on 1 teaspoon of the dried herb to make an infusion. Drink three cups a day. Alternatively, take 1–2ml of tincture three times a day.

Ulmus fulva

This fine powder has a long tradition of medicinal use by Native Americans.

Parts used – The inner bark is used, ground into a powder.

Indications – A soothing and nutritious remedy, this herb calms inflammation in the digestive system, helping ease colitis, acid indigestion, gastritis, and ulcers. It is a good food for convalescence, especially when other foods are difficult to digest.

Combinations – For digestive problems, combine slippery elm with marshmallow.

Cautions – If the stomach is very weak, add a small amount of clove, ginger, or fennel to aid digestion.

Dosages – Make a tea gruel with 6–10 grams of slippery elm powder and a cup of warm milk or water. Add honey or blackcurrant to sweeten if preferred.

Urtica dioica

This weed grows on wastelands, yet it is full of good nutrients.

Parts used – The leaves, stems, and flowers can be picked and used throughout its growing season. Use gloves when handling nettles.

Indications – Nettles are rich in vitamins and minerals, so they make a nourishing tonic, especially strengthening to those with weakness, debility, and anemia. They support and cleanse the liver and kidneys, clearing toxins and wastes. They are a beneficial treatment for childhood and nervous eczema.

Combinations – For a tonic, combine nettle and wild oat.

Dosages – Make a tea using 1–3 teaspoons of dried herb in one cup of boiled water and leave to infuse for 10–15 minutes. Drink three times a day. Alternatively, take 1–4 ml of tincture three times a day. The young tender leaves can be used to make a hearty soup.

Valeriana officinalis

This tall flowering plant, with its distinctive smell, flourishes near rivers and streams.

Parts used – The roots are collected in the late autumn and dried.

Indications – A wonderful remedy to relieve anxiety and muscular tension, valerian has a calming effect on the nervous system. It reduces symptoms of stress, is good for headaches, premenstrual syndrome, and sleeping difficulties. It is also antispasmodic and soothes cramps and period pains.

Combinations – For relief of tension and insomnia, combine valerian with skullcap and hops.

Dosages – Make a tea using 1–2 teaspoons of dried herb in one cup of boiled water and infuse for 10–15 minutes. Drink three times a day. Alternatively, take 2–4 ml of tincture three times a day.

Verbena officinalis

This delicate flower grows wild on roadsides and wasteland.

Parts used – The leaves and stems can be collected in the late spring before the flowers open.

Indications – Vervain strengthens the nervous system and relieves tension and anxiety. It eases depression and melancholy, especially following an illness. It is a gentle stimulant for the digestive system, useful for constipation, lethargy, and irritability. As a woman's remedy it brings on menstruation and promotes the flow of breast milk.

Combinations – For depression, combine vervain with skullcap and wild oats.

Cautions – Avoid vervain during pregnancy as it stimulates the uterus.

Dosages – Make a tea using 1–2 teaspoons of dried herb in one cup of boiled water and infuse for 10–15 minutes. Drink three times a day. Alternatively, take 2–4 ml of tincture three times a day.

Vitex agnus castus

Native to Mediterranean regions, this small tree has dark leaves and small purple flowers that give way to berries in the autumn. It is also known as chasteberry.

Parts used – The very dark berries can be picked in October or November, when ripe, then dried.

Indications – Agnus Castus stimulates and normalizes the pituitary gland, especially its progesterone function. It is used to steady the hormones during menopausal changes, helping with irregular periods, painful periods and premenstrual symptoms. It can also be used to help the body regain balance after using the contraceptive pill.

Combinations – This remedy combines well with other remedies for menopausal symptoms.

Dosages – Pour a cup of boiling water on 1 teaspoon of berries and infuse for 10–15 minutes. Alternatively, take 2–3 ml of tincture in a small amount of water each morning.

CHINESE HERBAL FORMULAS

Chinese herbal prescriptions are a combination of herbs based on traditional formulas. They are generally made into decoctions, which require the herbs to be soaked and cooked. Several manufacturers now make them as pills, which are convenient and easy to take, but not as strong. Manufacturers may give the pills different names, but the traditional formula on which they are based should be listed. Please consult a Chinese herbalist to make sure you take the appropriate remedy.

tian wang bu xin dan

Emperor of Heaven's Special Pill to Tonify the Heart

This calming formula can be used for anxiety, palpitations, and insomnia. It brings harmony to the body, mind, and spirit through balancing the water and fire. It is very helpful to those whose symptoms are accompanied by sensations of heat and restlessness.

yue ju wan

Escape Restraint Pill

This remedy encourages the movement of *qi*, or energy. It moves stagnation of *qi*, clearing phlegm, indigestion, and stifling sensations in the chest and abdomen. This formula is contraindicated if there is much weakness.

xiao yao san

Free and Easy Wanderer

A moving and tonifying prescription that makes an excellent remedy for premenstrual syndrome. It encourages the flow of *qi*, or energy, relaxing tension and stress, easing breast pain, bloating and irritability. Also strengthening for the digestion, it can treat gastric complaints and fatigue.

zhi gan cao tang

Honey-Fried Licorice Decoction

A tonic for the blood and *qi*, or energy, with its main focus on the heart and its spirit. It relieves symptoms of anxiety, palpitations, irritability, emaciation, and shortness of breath. As it is a warming formula, use it with caution if there are signs of heat, such as hot flushes or nightsweats.

yu ping feng san

Jade Screen Powder

This wonderful formula strengthens the immune system, preventing the onset of colds and flus. It can be taken when there are recurring colds and flus, spontaneous sweating, or sensitivity to drafts.

ban xia hou po tang

Pinellia and Magnolia Bark Decoction

A formula that promotes the movement of *qi*, or energy, and clears phlegm. It is very effective as a remedy for a stifling sensation in the chest, or phlegm in the throat that is difficult to clear. Do not use if there are signs of heat, flushed face, and a bitter taste in the mouth.

liu jun zi tang

Six Gentlemen's Decoction

A tonic for the digestion, this formula helps with complaints of bloating, indigestion, loose stools, and flatulence. Generally strengthening for the whole body, it relieves symptoms of tiredness, weakness, and lethargy.

liu wei di huang wan

Six Ingredient Pill with Rehmannia

A cooling and *yin*-enriching herb, it helps to relieve symptoms of soreness and weakness of the lower back, light-headedness, dizziness, and tinnitus. It eases irritability, dry mouth, and flushed complexion. It is a nourishing herb for those who have become depleted with long-term overworking, or for the elderly.

bu zhong yi qi tang

Tonify the Middle and Augment the Qi Decoction

A strengthening formula, especially for the digestion, it relieves symptoms of tiredness, lethargy, and fatigue. It helps those who have a tendency to feel the cold and want to withdraw and to curl up. It is an uplifting formula that can help with depression.

gui pi tang

Restore the Spleen Decoction

A tonifying and calming remedy that helps with anxiety, insomnia, and lack of concentration. Nourishing to the blood, it is recommended for those who are pale, and suffering from anemia. It also strengthens the digestion.

ba zhen wan

Women's Precious Pills

A good tonic for women, this remedy nourishes the blood and strengthens the *qi*, or energy. It is restoring when used following childbirth and after heavy menstrual bleeding. It is a helpful formula for tiredness, fatigue, and anemia.

BACH FLOWER REMEDIES

This system of healing, which has been Divinely revealed unto us, shows that it is our fears, our cares, our anxieties and such like that open the path to the invasion of illness. Thus by treating our fears, our cares, our worries and so on, we not only free ourselves from our illness, but the Herbs given unto us by the Grace of the Creator of all, in addition take away our fears and worries, and leave us happier and better in ourselves.

DR. EDWARD BACH

The 38 flower remedies discovered by Dr. Bach bring healing to the mind and emotions. These gentle remedies work on the subtle energy levels to restore balance and harmony within our soul. They offer a way of working with our fears, anxieties, and concerns, helping us along our journey of self-discovery, bringing understanding for ourself and others. Through bringing an awareness of our emotional patterns, and restoring peace within ourselves, we heal and prevent physical illness.

Bach Flower Remedies are safe for use on people of all ages – including children – and have no harmful side effects. The wrong choice of remedy will not do harm, it just will not be effective.

When reading through the list of remedies, it will seem that many could be useful. In choosing the most appropriate remedy for yourself, it is good to have a clear picture of what is needed. Take some time to try to understand your emotions and the patterns involved in the ways you deal with difficult situations. Meditate or reflect in a quiet space about your immediate problem and whether your reactions are appropriate or not. Choose up to five remedies to use in

combination to support the changes that are needed in yourself to bring about a positive state.

Taking these remedies will help to increase your self-awareness. You may find that a remedy will make you feel mentally or emotionally worse for a short while as you learn what is causing the disharmony within yourself. A release of emotions, although painful, can be the beginning of healing. The remedies can also have a very subtle reaction that may lead to a gradual awareness of changes in your reactions and emotions to situations. Take the same remedies for six to eight weeks, unless another remedy becomes strongly indicated or there is a change in circumstances.

Place two drops of the chosen remedy in a small amount of water. Sip at intervals throughout the day. Alternatively, fill a 20-ml dropper bottle with natural spring water (non-gas) and add two drops of the chosen remedies, using up to five remedies in one bottle. Add a small amount of brandy or cider vinegar (if you want to avoid alcohol) to preserve it. Take four drops on the tongue four times a day, especially first thing in the morning and before

bedtime at night. In crisis, take the prepared remedy as often as needed.

The remedies can be applied to wrists or foreheads if someone is unconscious or asleep, and they will be absorbed through the skin. They can be added to bath water or used as a spray in a room. They can also be used to treat plants and animals. Add two drops of the appropriate remedy to their food or water.

AGRIMONY
Agrimonia eupatori

For joyful, cheerful people who love peace and are distressed by quarrels and arguments. They hide their worries behind their good humor, and may resort to drugs and alcohol to keep up appearances and cope with problems and concerns. They do not like to burden others with their problems. This remedy works to clear suppressed emotions and bring a sense of peace and stillness through the resolution of conflict.

ASPEN
Populus tremula

For those with vague fears of unknown origin, a sense of foreboding, or terrors and nightmares that are often unexplainable. They may find it difficult to talk about these fears. This remedy brings an inner confidence and courage that calms such fears.

BEECH
Fagus sylvatica

For those who are critical and at times intolerant of situations. Perfectionists who are unable to see the good in others, and use this to create a false sense of security in themselves. This remedy brings tolerance and understanding of the different ways in which individuals work, a loving acceptance of life's imperfections.

CENTURY
Centaurium erythraea, c. umbellatum

For kind, gentle people who are overly anxious to serve and please others. They tend to work hard for others, finding it difficult to say "no." This remedy encourages strength and self-awareness so their own goals are remembered and held.

CERATO
Ceratostigma willmottianna

For the unconfident, who are continually seeking advice from others, rather than relying on their own wisdom. It helps those who want to move forward, but are bewildered by uncertainty, unable to discriminate between right and wrong, important and superficial decisions. This remedy brings focus within to see your own truths, and gives the confidence to trust your intuition.

CHERRY PLUM
Prunus cerasifera

For fearful, anxious people who lose control over their mind and emotions. Uncontrollable anger and terror, and suicidal thoughts indicate this remedy is needed. It brings a sense of harmony and calm to those who are desperate for this peace and yet cannot find it in themselves.

CHESTNUT BUD
Aesculus hippocastanum

For those who do not learn from observation and experience, and so repeat the same mistakes over again. This remedy brings alertness and interest into present circumstances so life's lessons can be learnt, encouraging new growth.

CHICORY
Cichorium intybus

For those who are mindful of the needs of others, and at times become correcting and manipulating. They can be possessive, demanding, and self-pitying while tending to others. This remedy brings a true devotion and service to humanity, one of compassion and selflessness.

Clematis vitalba

CLEMATIS

For dreamers not interested in their present circumstances, preferring to daydream and live in the future. In illness they make little effort to get better and may even look forward to death. This remedy offers stability, and brings the soul into a practical realm, teaching how to find support to make the dream into reality.

Malus pumila or sylvestris

CRAB APPLE

For those who feel they need cleansing, and may concentrate on this aspect of themselves obsessively. Self-disgust, shame, and low self-esteem, as well as physical infections are all indications for this remedy. It detoxifies and purifies the body, mind, and spirit, transforming negativity.

Ulmus procera

ELM

For hardworking people who are following their calling in life, but may at times feel overwhelmed and despondent about the amount of work there is to do. This remedy brings strength and conviction to fulfil the task at hand, reminding your soul of the support that is all around.

Gentiana amarella

GENTIAN

For those who are easily discouraged, when small setbacks lead to self-doubt, despondency, and depression. This remedy brings encouragement and the understanding that when you are doing your best, there is no failure, whatever the result.

Ulex europaeus

GORSE

For people who have lost hope, and believe nothing else can be done for them. Under persuasion they may try other treatments but they do not believe that anything will help. This remedy reminds that hope may grow faint, but never dies, and brings golden strength, certainty, and confidence.

Calluna vulgaris

HEATHER

For the lonely who need the company of others and want to discuss their affairs with anyone who will listen. They do not like to be left alone. This remedy calms fears and soothes the anxieties of those over-concerned with petty details. It helps to bring peace of mind, undisturbed by events, circumstances, or other people.

Ilex aquifolium

HOLLY

For those who are overcome by negative emotions such as anger, envy, and jealousy. They may suffer inside, often when there is no real cause for their unhappiness. This remedy transforms these emotions with love, gentleness, and compassion.

Lonicera caprifolium

HONEYSUCKLE

For those who live in the past, perhaps in happier times, or before the loss of a loved one. Not expecting further happiness in their lives, they are caught in nostalgia, homesickness, and reminiscing. This remedy focuses attention on the present, encouraging plunging back into life with the wisdom of past experiences.

HORNBEAM
Carpinus betulus

For those who are feeling weak mentally and physically, and are unable to deal with life's challenges. Everyday affairs feel difficult, so procrastinating and putting off tasks becomes a pattern. A "Monday morning" feeling, when the pressures of the coming day feel too much is a good indication for this remedy. This rememdy brings zest for learning and a desire to experience life fully, knowing it is an adventure.

IMPATIENS
Impatiens glandulifera

For quick thinking and acting people, who prefer tasks to be done without delay or hesitation. They find it difficult to be patient or work with people who are slower than them. They often prefer to work alone. This remedy carries gentleness, sweetness, and a relaxed tenderness, which clears impatience and irritation.

LARCH
Larix decidua

For people who are despondent, lack confidence, and expect failure, even though they possess the skills needed for the task at hand. They do not put themselves forward, so their fears become a self-fulfilling prophesy. This remedy builds confidence and brings awareness of capabilities, helping you to know truly that you can do it.

MIMULUS
Mimulus guttatus

For those who are afraid of everyday things – illness, pain, accidents, poverty, the darkness, or being alone. Timidity and shyness, and secretly bearing fears are good indictors that this remedy is needed. It helps to conquer fears, bringing confidence, trust, and joy of life.

MUSTARD
Sinapis arvensis

For despair and despondency, sadness, and gloom that comes over suddenly and for no reason at all. It takes over so strongly, like a black cloud, that they are not able to feel joy or happiness. This remedy brings the strength of brightness and cheerfulness that dispels the gloom and negativity.

OAK
Quercus robur

For those who are normally strong and fit, and unable to give up despite setbacks or illness. They go on trying one thing after another, fighting against great difficulties, without loss of hope or effort. This remedy helps them to accept limitations, share burdens, and develop a more balanced way of being in life.

OLIVE
Olea europaea

For people who have suffered and struggled with life, and are now exhausted both mentally and physically. Life seems hard and joyless. This remedy helps to unite body, mind, and spirit, so they work together. It gives strength, support, and comfort.

PINE
Pinus sylvestris

For those who blame themselves and feel guilty. Even with success, they find fault with themselves and feel they could have done better. They are hardworking and suffer much from the faults they find in themselves. Sometimes they will even take the blame for another person, claiming mistakes that are not theirs. This remedy brings the realization that they are perfect, loved, safe, and supported.

Aesculus carnea
RED CHESTNUT

For those who are over-concerned or anxious, especially around loved ones. They may fear for others' safety, health, and well-being, but often do not worry about themselves. This remedy transforms fear for loved ones, changing expressions of concern to those of support and confidence.

RESCUE REMEDY

This remedy is for emergencies and crisis, helping to calm emotions and clear trauma. It is useful for overcoming fearful situations, such as exams or interviews, and helps relieve the shock after accidents. It is a combination of remedies – impatiens, clematis, rock rose, cherry plum, and Star of Bethlehem.

Helianthemum nummularium
ROCK ROSE

For those experiencing terror, panic, hysteria, great fear, and nightmares. It is used in emergency situations, even when there appears to be no hope. It brings courage to win against great odds and mental clarity in the face of extreme fear.

ROCK WATER

For people who are very strict about their way of life, denying themselves joy and pleasure because they might interfere with their work. They want to be well and strong, and will do anything to be so, hoping to set an example to others. This remedy brings peace and understanding, broadening the outlook to include many ways of being. As water, it teaches adaptability and fluidity.

Scleranthus annuus
SCLERANTHUS

For those who suffer from indecision; unable to decide between two choices they vacillate between them. They are usually quiet people who do not share their difficulties with others and may be prone to mood swings. This remedy brings self-determination, focus, and action. Determination will grow, and fear of plunging into life soon disappears as they realize learning comes from every experience.

Ornithogalum umbellatum
STAR OF BETHLEHEM

For great distress following the shock of bad news, the loss of someone loved, or the fright of a serious accident. This remedy brings consolation, comfort, and peace.

Castanea sativa
SWEET CHESTNUT

For times of great anguish or distress, when the pain is almost unendurable, the limits of endurance have been reached, and nothing is left except dark despair. This remedy brings its exceptional life-force to carry you through the darkness, reminding you of courage and strength.

Verbena officinalis
VERVAIN

For people with strong ideas and fixed opinions, wanting to convert others to their own views of life. They have a strong will and much courage, but are often overenthusiastic and overpowering. When ill, their determination helps them to struggle on with their duties long after most would give up. This remedy encourages restraint and self-discipline, allowing the wider picture to unfold without stress or strain.

VINE

For capable people, confident of their own ability and success, certain they are right. They can be overbearing and dictatorial, directing others, even in their illness. This remedy helps to loosen their hold over others, so that love and compassion become the way of relating, and generous support is felt by all.

WALNUT

Juglans regia

For those who have definite ambitions and ideals, but may be distracted by others' opinions and actions. For times of change in life – puberty, starting a new job, marriage, moving home, or menopause. This remedy protects you from outside influences that stop them from following a chosen path.

WATER VIOLET

Hottonia palustris

For lonely, quiet people who prefer seclusion to the company of others. Often self-reliant and independent, they do not get involved in other people's affairs. They may appear proud and aloof. This remedy brings the joy of helpfulness, humility, and wisdom. Their peace and calmness is a blessing to those around them.

WHITE CHESTNUT

Aesculus hippocastanum

For people who cannot stop their thoughts from circling round and round, and become distracted by them. Their worries and preoccupation may become overbearing, a type of mental torture. The presence of such unpleasant thoughts drives out peace, preventing them from relaxing or concentrating. This remedy teaches calm thought and meditation, allowing the soul to be a guide.

WILD OAT

Bromus ramosus

For those who have great ambitions and experience, wanting to live life to the fullest. Their difficulty is to determine what occupation to follow, and this may cause frustration and dissatisfaction. This remedy helps determine their direction in life.

WILD ROSE

Rosa canina

For those who become resigned to life, and do not take any interest in present circumstances, making little effort to find happiness. For apathy and resignation where adverse influences take over, and joy of life is lost. This remedy brings delight, courage, vitality, and renewed hope that open them to life's richness.

WILLOW

Salix vitellina

For bitterness and resentment, and those who find it difficult to accept their misfortune. They feel such adversity is undeserved and unjust. They complain and become embittered, unable to enjoy their interests. This remedy brings a sense of resilient new growth, flexibility, and determination to overcome any obstacles.

RESOURCES

herbal remedies

Potters Herbal Supplies Ltd
Leyland Mill Lane
Wigan
Lancashire WN1 2SB
01942 234761

G. Baldwin & Co.
171-3 Walworth Road
London SE17 1RW
020 7703 5550

Neals Yard Remedies
15 Neals Yard
Covent Garden
London WC2H 9DP
020 7379 7222

Iden Croft Herbs
Fritenden Road
Staplehurst
Kent TN12 0DH
01580 891 432

Herbal Apothecary
103 High Street
Syston
Leicester LE7 1GQ
0116 260 2690

Culpepper Ltd
21 Bruton Street
Berkeley Square
London W1X 70A
020 7629 4559

Mayway (UK) Ltd
Unit 43, Waterside Trading
  Estate
Trumpers Way
Hanwell
London W7 2QD
020 8893 6873

Healthpack Ltd
East West Herbs (UK)
Langston Priory Mews
Kingham
Oxfordshire OX7 6UP
01608 658 816

The American Herbalists Guild
PO Box 1683
Soquel, California 95073
408 464 2441

Mountain Rose Herbs
20818 High Street
North San Juan, California 95960
800 879 3337
www.mountainroseherbs.com

Mayway (US)
1338 Cypress Street
Oakland, California 94607
510 208 3113
www.mayway.com

bach flower remedies

International Flower Essence
  Repertoire
The Living Tree
Milland
Liphook
Hampshire GU30 7JS
01428 741 572

Dr. Edward Bach Center
Mount Vernon, Bakers Lane
Sotwell
Wallingford
Oxfordshire OX10 0PZ
01491 834678

BIBLIOGRAPHY

Barnard, Julian. *Patterns of Life Force*, Flower Remedy Program, 1987

Barnard, Julian & Martine. *The Healing Herbs of Edward Bach*, Bach Educational Program, 1988

Bach, Edward. *The Twelve Healers*, Dr. Edward Bach Center, 1990

Bensky, Dan & Barolet, Randall. *Formulas and Strategies*, Eastland Press 1992

Bensky, Dan & Gamble, Andrew. *Materia Medica*, Eastland Press, 1993

Bremness, Lesley. *Pocket Encyclopedia, Herbs*, Dorling Kindersley, 1997

Bunney, Sarah. *The Illustrated Book of Herbs*, Octopus Books Ltd, 1984

Cohen, Misha Ruth. *The Chinese Way to Healing: Many Paths to Wholeness*, The Berkley Publishing Group 1996

Cowan, Eliot. *Plant Spirit Medicine*, Swan, Raven & Co., 1995

Culpepper, Nicholas. *Complete Herbal*, Omega Books, 1985

Frawley, David, Dr., & Lad, Vasant, Dr. *The Yoga of Herbs*, Lotus Press, 1986

Grieve, M. *A Modern Herbal*, Penguin Books, 1984

Hanh, Thich Nhat. *Peace Is Every Step*, Rider Book 1995

Hopman, Ellen Evert. *A Druid's Herbal*, Destiny Books, 1995

Hoffmann, David. *The New Holistic Herbal*, Barnes & Noble Books, 1995

Holmes, Peter. *The Energetics of Western Herbs*, Snow Lotus Press, 1997

HH Dalai Lama & Cutler, Howard, C. *The Art of Happiness*, Hodder & Stoughton, 1998

Jay, Roni. *Sacred Flowers*, Thorsons, 1997

Kircher, Tamara & Britton, Jade. *Herbal Remedies*, Marshall Publishing, 1998

Kircher, Tamara & Lowery, Penny. *Herbal Remedies*, Greenwich Editions, 1996

Linn, Denise. *Sacred Space*, Rider, 1995

Maciocia, Giovanni. *The Practise of Chinese Medicine* , Churchill Livingstone, 1994

McIntyre, Anne. *The Complete Floral Healer*, Gaia Books Ltd., 1996

McIntyre, Anne. *Herbs for Common Ailments*, Gaia Books Ltd., 1992

McIntyre, Michael. *Chinese Herbal Tonics*, East-West Press, 1986

Mojay, Gabriel. *Aromatherapy for Healing the Spirit*, Gaia Books Ltd., 1996

Myss, Caroline. *Why People Don't Heal and How They Can*, Bantam Books, 1998

Paterson, Jaqueline Memory. *Tree Wisdom*, Thorsons, 1996

Schefer, Mechthild. *Bach Flower Therapy*, Thorsons, 1986

Stapley, Christina. *Herb Sufficient*, Heartsease Books, 1998

Trungpa, Chögyam. *Shambhala*, Shambhala Dragon Editions, 1998

Walsh, Roger. *Essential Spirituality*, John Wiley & Sons, 1999

INDEX

HERBS FOR THE SOUL